fUn WiTh fReD

LIFE WITH OCD
AND HOARDING

A HUMOROUS MEMOIR

Leslie Robinson

ISBN 979-8-9869452-0-0 (paperback)

ISBN 979-8-9869452-1-7 (e-Book)

Book cover and design by Laura Boyle Design

To all my fellow sufferers. May you learn to put your Fred in his place: six feet under.

Introduction

My obsessive-compulsive disorder, which is called Fred, causes me to doubt constantly. Even so, I'll declare with what feels to me like impetuous abandon the following: You'll get something out of this book.

What, exactly, depends on who you are.

If you have OCD, or if you have what's now called hoarding disorder, or if you happen to be weighted down with both, this book affirms that you're far from alone.

If you're trying to figure out whether you suffer from either of these conditions, this book helps you arrive at answers.

If you have a family member or a friend who's afflicted, this book gives you a glimpse of what's happening in your loved one's head, which could be especially useful if you're currently feuding like Bugs Bunny and Yosemite Sam.

If you're generally curious about these illnesses, and have seen them represented in movies and TV, and have no idea what could compel someone to check the front door 17 times or keep every twist tie since 1980, this book conveys a little of what science knows, and a lot of the white-hot anxiety that makes people like me do the odd things we do.

If you simply like to read memoirs about folks who are different, this book fits the bill.

After reading this book, if you decided you didn't get anything out of it, feel free to tell me. Just know that when you do, I'll obsess over this failure for the rest of my life.

No pressure.

If you did get something out of this book, feel free to tell me that, too. These disorders cause mighty struggles, and I'll be pleased if I helped you in yours.

It won't make up for all I've gone through—let's not be ridiculous. But I hope telling my story will advance and encourage understanding of these disorders. I can't get decades back, but I can use the time I still have to smooth the path for others with the same burdens.

If this sure as hell wasn't the plan for my life, it's now an excellent use of it. And if I can do something that aggravates assorted Freds out there, well, hurray.

Author's Note

I've changed a few names. But definitely not Fred's.

Chapter 1

The psychiatrist suggested I give my disorder a name. An odd suggestion, but not nearly as odd as the condition itself, so I didn't quibble. At our next session I announced my decision. My obsessive-compulsive disorder would be called Fred.

I immediately regretted the choice. Fred Mertz appeared in my head, one of the happy associations I have with that name. I sighed, and hoped he and Fred Astaire wouldn't be tainted.

I hadn't pondered the decision much. "Fred" came to me quickly, automatically. Over a decade later, I believe that's because the name sounds heavy and unyielding, like a block of cement. It's a thud of a name.

Plus "Fred" is so close to "fret," and when you have OCD, fretting is your primary activity.

So Fred it was. And Fred it still is.

Chapter 2

The psychiatrist thought I needed to grasp that I'm not the OCD. Give the disorder a name, and you're better able to see it as separate from you, experts say.

Then you can see OCD as the brain-wasting, time-sucking, life-demolishing fiend it is.

Experts don't say that. Actually, the good ones do.

In my better moments it's clear to me that I'm a person with a disorder, as opposed to being the disorder. On those favored occasions I imagine the OCD floating near me, a leaden gray cloud not far from my head.

But for the most part, despite personifying my condition, separating myself from it remains a tall order. For one thing, Fred is always with me. He lives inside my head, the guest who wouldn't leave. Nor did he ever bring a hostess gift.

Fred has affected my life so profoundly, and I feel so much shame about him, that it's a gargantuan struggle for me to separate us. He and I are bound together in a lifelong game of Twister.

Not that our version of the game is any fun. Obsessive-compulsive disorder is nobody's idea of a good time.

Simply put, obsessions are persistent thoughts that cause excessive worry. Compulsions are repetitive behaviors performed to allay those worries.

This might sound like the ideal disorder—you get anxious, but you can calm yourself through behaviors. How efficient.

OCD doesn't work that way. You have to repeat the behavior over and over to achieve peace, and the peace is temporary. The obsessive thought will be back. Fred wouldn't dream of leaving me alone for even a little while. He's loyal that way.

For years I've identified myself as a checker and a hoarder. OCD has a breathtaking number of manifestations, and I've learned that checking and hoarding aren't my only forms of Fred, but they're the two most acute.

I promise you that right now, in order to rid himself of a sense of dread, somebody in your town is checking one of the following: stove, coffee maker, refrigerator, iron, thermostat, fireplace, front door, window lock, hair dryer, electric toothbrush, outlet, computer, printer, cell phone, TV, car ignition or you.

A hoarder is telling herself to hold onto some old, rusty wire, because you just never know when it might come in handy.

Sure it will—the next time she has a hankering to contract tetanus.

OCD doesn't trump logic; it swamps it. A tidal wave of anxiety knocks rational thought on its keister.

OCD sufferers who don't grapple with my twin bugaboos of checking and hoarding experience other versions of the disorder. Consider the basic types of OCD listed in "The OCD Workbook," a self-help guide for the afflicted.

There are washers and cleaners, whose fear of contamination has them repeatedly washing their hands, showering or cleaning their homes.

Then we have the orderers and repeaters, who must arrange items in a precise way, or repeat words or actions over and over. Folks with scrupulosity obsess over religious or ethical matters. Others endure horrible thoughts of violently harming people, or acting on unwanted sexual impulses.

Throw in checking and hoarding, and it's safe to say this disorder is loaded with variety.

While scanning "The OCD Workbook," I noticed a section for parents of children with OCD. It seems that the technique of giving your condition a name is most often used with kids. I could worry that a psychiatrist told me to do it when I was 37, but I already have enough to worry about.

Give your child's OCD a name to help "externalize" it, the book advises, suggesting such evocative options as "Mr. Worry, Mrs. Clean, Washy, Mr. Gooey, Checkers, and The Count." If the descriptive monikers don't suit, the authors suggest "Fred, Sam, Pete, Molly, or Jane."

Fred. I picked a name that a lot of people might be picking, thanks to the self-help book suggesting it. My sense of originality chafes at having chosen something potentially overused.

Oh well. Fred and I are stuck together forever. I realize now that one of the other suggestions, Jane, would've worked for me, too, with a tweak. I could've gone with a name that reflects the worry that's at the heart of OCD: Calamity Jane.

Chapter 3

Worry.

It's the reason I haven't written a word of this book for two weeks.

When I think about sitting down and working on it a big knot of anxiety leaps into my stomach. That hunk o' nerves is enough to keep me from the task. I don't stop and ask myself what I'm nervous about. Fred has me so well trained that I don't think. I feel that anxiety knot and I either make it go away by avoiding the task, or I do the task scared.

Neither seems like a recipe for success.

I'm putting the question to myself right here, right now: Why am I afraid of working on this book?

I worry that I won't describe my symptoms accurately. Or my experiences. Or my memories. I worry that I'll leave out important parts of the story. I worry that I'll make factual errors on statistics and psychological theory. I worry that my sources aren't the most up-to-date.

That's what my stomach knot is telling me. It has a lot to say.

Speaking of stomachs, I won't go to the computer if I'm the least bit hungry. That's out of fear that hunger pangs will muddle my thinking.

I also won't go to the computer unless I know I have a chunk of time available. I need the time to write, of course. More than that, I need extra time to cope with the overwhelming doubt that accompanies the writing process and slows it excruciatingly. Have I left something out? Is that precisely what I mean?

Even though I want to tell my story, even though at this point in my life I need to tell my story, I approach the computer as enthusiastically as I'd approach a rabid gnu.

Chapter 4

So let's get on with the statistics I'm terrified of misunderstanding or citing inaccurately or otherwise bastardizing. Sounds like fun, no?

According to "The OCD Workbook," OCD is the fourth most common psychiatric diagnosis in the United States. Up to 2.5 percent of Americans have it, which translates to one out of every 40 people.

Bang goes my desire to be original.

Actually, knowing that over 6.6 million people in this country might be in this leaky boat with me is reassuring. I'm not alone. Not even close.

I have company the world over, as it happens. OCD exists in every nation. My Fred is someone else's Friedrich or Federico. Or Indira or Chin Ho or Rashid.

Among adults in the U.S., women are a tad more likely to have OCD than men, but among children, boys have it at about twice the rate of girls.

Apparently girls catch up. Rats. This is one area where I could've done without equality.

The "Diagnostic and Statistical Manual of Mental Disorders," published by the American Psychiatric Association, is the Bible of the mental-health field. The most recent version, the DSM-IV-TR, published in 2000, explains that for males OCD tends to set in between ages six and 15. For females the curse generally descends between ages 20 and 29.

In the interest of accuracy—and you might've gleaned that's a concern of mine—I'll mention that the DSM suggests the figure of 2.5 percent of Americans with OCD could be too high, owing to "methodological problems with the assessment tool used."

Because I've grown to like the idea of having lots of company in my leaky boat, I say we ignore this.

The DSM also notes that most people experience a gradual onset of OCD. But some folks wake up one day and realize they can't go another minute without alphabetizing their condiments.

Chapter 5

Oh. My. God.

My partner Anne and I attended a talk today given by a psychologist. It turns out that a new edition of the DSM is coming out in six months, and the changes concerning OCD will be profound.

I'm a wreck. Fred's ecstatic.

Just as I've set myself the task of explaining OCD, the very definition has changed. I feel like I'm slipping on a cosmic banana peel.

For starters, OCD might not even be classified as an anxiety disorder any longer. I can't say what its new classification might be, because Anne and I arrived late to the talk, and for the record, we were late because she got caught up in a task, not because I was embroiled in an extravaganza of checking. So there.

What did become clear is that, in the next version of the DSM, hoarding will be separated out from OCD. It's about to be its own disorder, hoarding disorder.

This means I now have not one but two disorders! My cup runneth over. With sewage.

I haven't changed, but in a flash my mental illnesses doubled. I'm now officially twice the mess I was yesterday. I'd like to give the American Psychiatric Association a piece of my mind. Not that I can spare it.

Since I was diagnosed with OCD twenty years ago, I've battled the twin evils of checking and hoarding. The two defined me as a person with OCD. After all these years of being labeled and labeling myself, now I'm not sure who I am.

Fred knows, but that isn't remotely reassuring.

Like many with OCD, I'm allergic to change. It offers Fred too many opportunities to stir up anxiety. My understanding of my world is being forced to change. Fred knows all this and sees one thing: Party!

Something just occurred to me. If OCD and hoarding are two separate issues, and I call my OCD Fred, do I need to come up with a name for my hoarding?

At the moment, drag names leap to mind. Lotte Stuff. Miss Accumulate. Blythe Lee Accruing.

No. I'm going to use Fred to cover both conditions. Unless some expert tells me I shouldn't, in which case I'll choose a name that partners well with Fred. Like Ginger.

Chapter 6

Days later, at a Thai restaurant, Anne listened while I bemoaned the changes in the DSM. "I think it's for the greater good," she said, in an appalling burst of disloyalty.

People who hoard but don't check or show other signs of OCD may get more appropriate treatment now that hoarding is its own diagnosis, she opined.

I didn't recall ordering a side of logic with my red curry.

Anne said the DSM evolves as our medical understanding evolves, and she reminded me that homosexuality was listed as a mental illness in the DSM until 1973.

Thank heavens it's not there anymore. Otherwise I'd have a total of three disorders. That would be positively gaudy.

Anne noted that for hoarders, OCD sufferers and others with anxiety disorders, "the common hitchhiker is depression."

Yes, depression frequently does accompany anxiety disorders. Yes, I've been diagnosed with depression. Yes, when the new DSM comes out I'll fit into three categories. Yes, color me gaudy.

Chapter 7

The DSM I'm using, the one now galloping toward obsolescence, defines OCD this way:

> The essential features of Obsessive-Compulsive Disorder are recurrent obsessions or compulsions that are severe enough to be time consuming (i.e., they take more than 1 hour a day) or cause marked distress or significant impairment. At some point during the course of the disorder, the person has recognized that the obsessions or compulsions are excessive or unreasonable. I meet all the criteria. Boy howdy do I.

I experience obsessions, anxiety-producing notions, all day long, every day, and I try to put the kibosh on the fear by performing a compulsion, by checking. This process devours time. I think I've even heard burps.

The obsessions cause me loads of distress. If they didn't, they wouldn't be called "obsessions," but rather "thoughts that are here, then they're gone, pfft." I perform the compulsions precisely because the obsessive thoughts send my anxiety into the stratosphere.

The obsessions and compulsions impair me plenty, both personally and professionally. And I'm only too aware that checking the contents of the garbage can 15 times is not the most valuable use of my time, mind or master's degree.

But that doesn't mean I can stop. The obsessions and compulsions are more powerful than dung beetles, and possessed of equal charm.

Chapter 8

I just put the garbage out. I'm pretty sure I threw out the Crown Jewels.

Or my passport, or my checkbook, or something vital to my existence. I don't get specific in my worry. Every week, after putting the garbage bin in front of the house, I walk away with a blanket sense of dread that I've tossed out something important.

I'd give a lot to be able to walk away knowing that I've thrown out only things that should go out, or better yet, not to care.

That won't happen while Fred's on the case. His most distinctive quality is his persistence.

Putting out the garbage is easy for someone without OCD. It's the time-honored task assigned to teenagers because it involves no thought and a strong back. I have a weak back and I think about garbage far more than garbage deserves.

Starting with when I first gather it. Before pulling the kitchen garbage bag from its container, I stare at the contents and think "kitchen trash." Then I go to the bathroom, empty its little trashcan into the kitchen garbage bag and think "bathroom trash."

With this mantra I'm reassuring myself that I'm throwing out trash, not, say, fine art. It works for a couple more rooms, but it loses its potency by the time I reach the other bathroom. After emptying that trashcan into the big bag, my festival of checking begins.

I eyeball the contents. I shift the bag to see more. "There's the kitchen trash, the office trash, the bathroom trash," I tell myself, as I spot the garbage from each room. If this reduces the anxiety, I leave the bathroom. If not, I perform more rounds of reassurance, possibly saying the words out loud: "Kitchen, office, bathroom."

I sound like a possessed real estate agent.

It could be that I lean in and touch some of the items, going for tactile reassurance. When I reach the point of touching potentially icky things, Fred does a happy dance.

Usually I achieve some measure of lowered anxiety, and I leave the room. When the anxiety is still strong despite all the checking, I eventually leave anyway. I'd say I have no choice, but I recall a story on TV about a young man with OCD who couldn't leave his bathroom. I assume he feared germs—which means he'd never have accepted garbage duty in the first place.

After adding the contents of the trashcans downstairs, I escort the bag outside. I take the top off the garbage bin. I hold the bag up and stare at it, spinning it around until I recognize through the plastic an item that was definitely garbage. That means it's all garbage. Then I place the bag inside the garbage bin. Carefully, because catching the bag on the edge of the bin makes my anxiety shoot up, and I'll have to pull the bag out and check it again.

I carry the bin up to the curb and put it down. There's plenty of doubt in my gut, but I walk away. These days I draw the line at pulling the bag out and massaging it in front of the neighbors.

Anne and I don't amass that much garbage—even if describing going room to room makes it sound like I collect enough to fill Lake Erie—because eco-conscious Seattle emphasizes composting and recycling. Which means I have to grapple with Fred to get two more bins to the curb.

We keep a small compost bucket by our kitchen sink, and whenever it's full I dump the contents into a paper grocery bag and immediately rush that bag outside to deposit it into the food and yard waste bin.

You might assume I hustle the paper bag out so it won't stink up the kitchen. That's a perfectly reasonable thing to assume, and I forgive your ignorance. In fact, my main reasons are Fred-related. Delaying departure could cause all manner of catastrophes. Silverware could leap in the bag and never be seen again.

On the eve of pick-up, I roll the food and yard waste bin to the curb. After, of course, having opened it and stared inside to convince myself that only food waste and yard waste are inside. I have my standards. Or Fred's standards.

Then there's the recycling. We generate a lot of it, so one prowl through the house the night before pick-up isn't feasible. Instead, when the recycling containers in the kitchen or offices or bathrooms become bountiful, I tip the contents into a paper bag and head outside.

I throw open the flap of the recycling bin, lift up the paper bag . . . and don't chuck it in. No indeed. If I did, Fred would scream bloody murder as I walked away.

No, to head off that level of anxiety, I pick out each item from the bag, look at it briefly, hear "Yes" and then drop it in the bin. That "Yes" translates to "Yes, this piece of paper really should go out." Along with "Yes, I know it's nuts to worry so much about an empty black bean can."

When I'm disposing of the recycling from my office, I can toss a few items at once into the recycling bin, rather than just one at a time. I assume this recklessness is due to the fact that I already vetted the hell out of each item before placing it in the office's recycling container in the first place.

It's a different story when getting rid of the recycling from the kitchen or bathroom. The reason? Anne. Heaven knows what she's pitched.

We've been together over five years, so she's gotten to know Fred well. And vice versa—Fred is happily aware that on occasion Anne throws out something she shouldn't, so he has me checking on her closely.

Anne knows to be careful. She learned the hard way. Early on she tossed out a few items—meaning some form of paper that belonged to me—and each time my rage equaled that of Jesus in the Temple. But without his moral authority.

I didn't overturn tables, but I banged my hand on one and shrieked. I got her attention, and my own. Can a person who panics and seethes at the sudden loss of an old newspaper be in a relationship? Should she be?

Now Anne makes an effort not to toss out anything of mine during her bouts of tidiness. When I'm outside putting recycling into the bin and I find something she shouldn't have disposed of, I naturally tell her she's committed a sin, to which she replies, "I try not to throw your stuff out. But I'm only human." I agree with her, and the matter is finished. Officially. What I'm thinking is, "Cut out that being human shit! It doesn't work for me!"

So, after all this careful shepherding of the household's recycling into the recycling bin outside, I roll it up to the curb the night before collection. I won't add anything to it or the other two bins at this point, because that would fire up the need to check what's already on the curb.

The next day I listen attentively for the rumble of the disposal trucks. Now that I've gotten everything in position, I want it gone, gone, gone. The longer the stuff is out there, the more opportunity I have to obsess over it.

The other day I was walking the dogs and as I neared the house I spotted the compost truck stopping in front of it. I turned my back and let Red and Blue sniff a patch of greenery exhaustively, just so I wouldn't see the men dump our bin into the truck. If I'd watched, my anxiety that something important had gone out would've skyrocketed. I would've felt an impulse to run after the compost truck and root through the yard waste and food scraps. And that would've made the dogs jealous.

Chapter 9

Let's talk about the washing machine. I hear other people throw their laundry into it, add detergent, set the dials and walk away.

What a concept.

My approach is different. After gathering everything to be washed, I sort the laundry into piles of darks, lights and whites. I load the first pile into the washer, item by item so nothing of the wrong color creeps in, and check that all pockets are empty.

I used to examine each piece of laundry to see whether it had a stain that called for treating, but I've loosened up on that somewhat. I'm sure the makers of Shout are sorry to hear it.

Then I close the washer door, listening for the click that means it's really shut. Next I turn my attention to the settings. After deciding between Permanent Press and Regular/Cotton, I turn the dial to the correct water temperature. But is it the correct one? I return the dial to the starting point. I reassure myself it was the right one, and turn it back again.

I go back and forth several more times, trying to make the doubt go away. Someday I'll give the washing machine a nervous breakdown.

This machine doesn't have too many settings, thank God, so next it's time for the detergent. I prefer to add precisely the right amount, but lately I've been inexact. The reason is Anne bought some mega-sized detergents that pour messily into their measuring caps, causing stickiness all over the bottle and my hands and surfaces, so now I forego the measuring cap and pour the detergent directly into the detergent slot. Yup, I'm a wild woman.

This is actually an example of one hang-up beating another. I hate the mess more than I hate measuring inexactly. The only one who wins in this situation is Fred: What could be better than inflicting two fears at once? Double the fun.

Once I've poured the detergent in, I stare at it. I ask myself, Did I pour it in? Is it there? Even if it's plainly glistening at me, I'm still shockingly capable of doubting that I poured the stuff in. I might even stick a finger in to check.

Eventually I feel either sufficiently confident or sufficiently worn out, and I drop the flap over the detergent compartment. I walk away from the washing machine. Before I hit the stairs and make my escape, a solid block of doubt wallops me. I might return to recheck everything. Or I might force myself up the stairs, carrying the doubt with me.

For me laundry isn't just a chore. It's a CHORE.

Fred demands I put such careful effort into a basic exercise like laundry to minimize the possibility of mistakes. I check the water temperature because if I use the wrong one the clothes won't get clean, and then what will have been the point of doing laundry? If you're going to do something, do it right. Do it perfectly.

Fred's a bastard.

Despite my best efforts, I periodically prove that I'm not capable of being perfect. Consider that one of Anne's white athletic socks, which I accidentally tossed in a colored load, is now the color of a ripening raspberry.

Before Anne and I got together, I lived in an apartment building whose laundry room was next to my apartment. I could hear when people were in the laundry room, and I tried to use it when nobody else was around, giving myself the time to perform all my checking unobserved.

All too often, though, someone would walk in and catch me *in flagrante de-checko.* They wouldn't know I'd been pushing and re-pushing on the dryer's coin slot to check that all my quarters had indeed dropped through. But I'd know, and my anxiety would surge because I couldn't finish reassuring myself that all was as it should be.

With a friendly smile on my face, but a volcano in my stomach, I'd exit the laundry room, open my apartment door, step in, shut the door, turn around, close my eyes and review in my head every step of the laundry process I'd just taken.

On the fly, I shifted the location of my checking, and I did it all mentally, without props. I guess you could call that being resourceful. In a seriously pathetic sort of way.

When Anne and I became a duo, I happily did my laundry at her house. (No quarters! No rude interruptions!) On one occasion I carried all our clean clothes upstairs to the guestroom and dumped them on the bed, Anne's usual location for folding. Then she suggested we fold them later.

Whoa. What? Later? Not now? Is that legal?

I unhappily relented to this breaking of my rules, to this . . . this . . . change. That day my mind returned often to the laundry strewn across the guest bed, wantonly unfolded and vulnerable to cat hair and other miscellaneous types of debris that could've tidal-waved onto the clothes the minute I turned my back.

I live in a world of threats that would cow Sigourney Weaver.

Chapter 10

We interrupt our story to bring you breaking news. I just took a bag of recycling outside, and discovered that Anne had pitched the Sunday magazine before I got a chance to look at it.

Her body will never be found.

Chapter 11

When the letter carrier sticks our mail through the slot in the front door, the mail drops to the floor. I pick it up and sort it into two piles, one for Anne and one for me.

My pile will sit there for an hour. Or a week. Or a year.

I have unopened mail in my possession that dates to the era of the first President Bush. I don't discriminate—I ignore both my junk mail and my real mail. I've left bills unopened, which has led to financial predicaments. I've left letters and Christmas cards unopened, which has led to injured feelings.

Why do I manage, or mismanage, my mail like this?

I'm scared of it.

I'm fearful of dealing with the stuff. Every piece is a weight. A responsibility. A chance to screw up.

You'd think that junk mail would be easier to get rid of than regular mail, and it is. But that doesn't mean I can just toss it into the recycling and feel as free as Julie Andrews on an Alp.

I have to open that piece of junk mail to see that it's really what I think it is and that I don't need it. After all, the secret to spiritual enlightenment, or at least cheaper car insurance, could be inside that No. 10 envelope.

Real mail is scarier. If I open that bill, I could lose it. I could so lose it, somehow. If I open it, I'll have to pay it, and the process of paying a bill includes its own festival of Fred. When I'm low on money, I'm even less likely to open the bill, so I won't feel the jangle of nerves over how to pay it. No, better to leave the envelope right there by the door, unopened, unsullied, in plenty of company.

I'll open it later, when I can handle it. And that will be when pigs snorkel.

Even a happy piece of mail sparks fear. I'm so pleased to get a card from a friend that I'll . . . leave it sitting there for days. Because to open it is to have to deal with it.

I'll need to respond to the person, via card or phone or email, and my response must be high quality—if not scintillating, at least amusing. I'll also need to check that the return address on this envelope is precisely what I have in my address book. I'll waffle: Should I keep this card or throw it out? So many steps required, so many mistakes I could make, I'll leave it till later.

I don't think any of this when I retrieve the mail off the floor. I've been ignoring my mail for so long I don't think about it at all. It's second nature to just stack it and flee. I'm automatically keeping fear away.

I'm as well trained as a Labrador. But Fred never gives treats. He believes in the terror method of training. As I approach the scattered mail he installs a knot of fear in my stomach that means if I open just one letter the result will be general catastrophes and unspecified mayhem.

Fred conveys a lot with a little.

I should wear a scarlet A on my chest. Not for adulterer—for avoider. I feel the fear or the doubt, and I spring into inaction. I avoid what makes me nervous. I don't open that mail: I stack it till the pile collapses or Anne has a tizzy, whichever comes first.

I'm guilty of avoidance when it comes to my electronic mail, as well. If I don't feel I can handle a particular email at that moment, I won't open it. I'm convinced that I really will attend to it later. Sometimes that's true, sometimes that isn't. Looking at my email now, which stretches back over seven years, I see plenty of them are still in bold, meaning I haven't opened them.

I have exactly 3,000 emails in my account. I assume that's a lot. I assume that's ridiculous, even for an account that receives both personal and professional mail. In addition to the perpetually unread messages, I have a ton of read messages that I just haven't deleted, because they're work-related and I feel all work emails need to be kept; or they have information in them I might need; or they concern social gatherings that have long–since happened, but since I didn't delete them at the time, they must have some sort of importance.

If that logic were any more twisted, you could slather it with mustard and serve it in Central Park.

What I'm doing is hoarding. Both my physical mail and virtual mail I won't let go of without a fight, and that's due to an irrational but consuming fear that I'll lose something critical.

Thanks, Fred. Thanks a bunch.

Not surprisingly, the fact that I sometimes avoid opening email gets me into trouble. I irk Anne when I don't open something she sends that day. Worse than irk, actually. "It makes me very sad and hurt," she said recently, not least because she's selective in what she sends. The last thing I want to do is hurt her. Fred, on the other hand, is hunky-dory with that.

By the way, if you're wondering why I have precisely 3,000 emails in my inbox, it's not that Fred insists I maintain a round number. It's because when I reached that many, even I got sick of myself and vowed not to let the number grow. So when I receive new email that I can't handle in the moment, I go back and delete older messages. Either unread ones that really are unnecessary at this point, or read ones that I check for usefulness before deleting.

Because God forbid I just delete an email without checking it. I stand a better chance of sailing the Pacific Ocean on a No. 10 envelope.

Chapter 12

Here in my office, my desk faces the wall. I sit in an office chair that rolls. I can roll side to side well enough, but I can't roll backwards. The wheels aren't wonky. I am.

A thick impenetrable mass resides right behind me, consisting of stacks of newspaper, boxes of mail and reams of paperwork. This heap is a hymn to my hoarding. The accumulations cover most of the office floor, and have since I moved in with Anne four years ago.

Beyond the mounds, a large bookcase stands against the wall. I can't get at the books, not without performing contortions no middle-aged body should attempt.

There sit my books, so near and yet so near.

If I have a choice, I don't let people see this room. Sometimes it's unavoidable, like when a friend wants a tour of the house, in which case I'll rush her by the office while cracking, "Someday I'll actually move in."

The next thing I do during this grand tour is wave my arm vaguely at a closed door on the other side of the hall, offering nothing more informative than, "That's my large closet." I'm telling my friend the truth. What I'm omitting is the closet is jam-packed full of stuff, and I'd rather break into the bunny hop to distract her than open the door and let her see inside.

The closet does actually contain clothes, along with other legitimate items like DVD's and an ironing board and a blow-up bed. But there are also piles of magazines and newspapers. And then there are the boxes. Stacks of them. I mailed them here a few years ago, full of the last accumulations I still had at my mother's house thousands of miles away.

I'm a bicoastal hoarder.

These boxes are loaded with everything from books to college memorabilia to my childhood stuffed animals. I avoided sorting through all this when I lived back East, but I told myself if I mailed it out here I'd have the time and motivation to go through it. Some hoarders pour money into storage lockers. Me, I've been doing my bit to keep the U.S. Postal Service afloat.

So there sit the boxes, buried under scattered clothes. I haven't sorted their contents—hell, I haven't even opened them. Making decisions on what to keep feels too scary.

Hoarders can go out of their way to acquire things, picking up free magazines, carting home goodies from the dump or shopping excessively. I don't. I have my hands full with whatever comes to me naturally, like mail and the daily newspaper and grocery-store receipts. I won't let go of these things without being 6,000 percent sure I don't need them.

I shudder to think what life would be like if I deliberately acquired things as well. The house would be so packed I'd never find anything. Including Anne.

Chapter 13

I went on a treasure hunt this morning. I recently discovered my credit card had expired, so today I searched the piles on my office floor to uncover the replacement card the bank surely sent me months ago. I found the paperwork that came with the card, but no card.

Perhaps at some point I decided to put it in a safe place. Like Luxembourg.

Chances are the card is in one of these piles, because I add things to them still believing, against all evidence, that I'll deal with them soon. If I add to an existing hillock a handful of mail that I know includes bills or other important items, I tell myself that I'll have to deal with that handful. I'll have no choice. The stuff is critical. I can't ignore it.

I underestimate myself. I not only ignore it, within a few days I've forgotten about it. That takes skill.

If I have a pile of newspapers that Anne wants removed from the living room, I might drop it right next to my office chair, on the assumption that making my chair hard to reach means I'll be forced to comb through the newspapers.

No. The pile just becomes part of my office's topography. And I look like a Flying Wallenda trying to get into my chair.

During my fruitless search for the credit card I relearned three things. The first is black pants are a mistake for any archaeological dig. Excavation is dusty work.

The second is, though I shouldn't be, I'm always shocked at how much stuff I've accumulated. I combed through one box in a state of disbelief at all the mail, magazines, programs, ticket stubs and other printed material Fred and I have socked away.

But could I throw any of it out on the spot? Certainly not. The realization of how much crap I have stings, but the fear of getting rid of it stings more.

The third fact with which I became reacquainted this morning is that when I can't find something important and have to search through so many haystacks, I inevitably swear to the heavens that I'll never put myself in this situation again.

"Go through these piles, Leslie!" I chant. "Deal with your mail the day it arrives!"

The heavens get a good laugh.

Chapter 14

Last night I experienced one dream after another. First I had agreed to host some visitors who declined to leave, which rolled into a dream about trying to pay for groceries but never reaching the cash register, which rolled into a dream about being unable to find a hotel.

The unbroken cycle of dreaming and the consistent theme of frustration leave me in no doubt. I experienced at night what I'm experiencing during the day, utter frustration at the pace with which I'm writing this book.

Listen, if a person with OCD says she's sure about something, she is sure. To have no doubts? As rare as an Amish astronaut.

It remains a daily struggle to get myself to work on this project. Sure, I can take out the recycling or do the laundry—with certain attendant challenges. Yes, I can sit at the computer and check my email—to a point—or find funny stuff online to post on my gay humor blog. Of course, I can walk the dogs or toil in the garden. Naturally, I go to my part-time jobs.

But nothing is harder than sitting my rear in this chair and opening the folder on the computer and working. This isn't writer's block; it's a Fred blockade.

As I mentioned, I don't feel I can write until I've gotten other tasks out of the way, and I must have a chunk of time, and not be sick or hungry or tired. Writing itself is agonizing, as I crawl through a chapter, worrying over normal writerly elements like structure and clarity, and also worrying excessively, lavishly, monotonously over accuracy.

In short, Fred inspires such anxiety in me when I think of writing that I don't even start.

Which brings me to the paradox of this project: I want to write about Fred, but I can't write because of Fred.

If I believed in God, I'd have a chat with him about his sense of humor.

So I don't write and it eats at me, day and night. I have plenty of reasons to write this book—such as the chance to show friends and strangers what living with OCD is like, and to lord it over Fred—but whether I'll be able to pull this off is a crapshoot.

A further irony is I feel so good after writing. It's a release, describing the gorilla on my back, and any writer, with or without OCD, knows what a pleasure it is to convey something in a way that feels exactly right.

Even that incentive isn't enough. More often than not, fear beats the prospect of feeling good, and I don't write. But I'm not giving up. I'm going to keep fighting the anxiety, keep striving to get the words out.

Fred and I are going to the mat. If you're reading this, it means I pinned the SOB.

Chapter 15

Nearly a year has passed since I wrote those words. Between then and now you would've gotten very bad odds on my defeating Fred in our wrestling match. In fact, it must've looked like I'd hung up my singlet and gone home.

What happened? I got married. The wedding was a sizeable affair, requiring a lot of preparation. A couple of months before the August nuptials I felt I had to put this book aside.

Organizing your wedding? An acceptable excuse.

After the wedding, I needed some time to recover from all the effort and hoopla. An acceptable excuse.

In the fall I changed jobs, and Anne and I prepared for our Christmas honeymoon in Germany. An acceptable excuse and an acceptable excuse.

Then things veered to the unacceptable.

I returned home in January to my grand plan of working at my office job each morning, and working on this book and my blog each afternoon. For months I managed the job and the blog, but instead of writing the book, I wrote a guide to my job, an old habit whenever I began new employment. Working for a small business that serves the financial and medical needs of seniors, I had a lot to learn, and thus, a lot to write.

I wanted the guide to be accurate and thorough. Consequently I wrote at a pace that would embarrass a snail.

Fred was in his glory. He required the guide to be perfect, so it took forever to finish, which kept me from working on the book. Since the book, too, has to be perfect, part of me was happy never going near it, while the other part stewed over time passing.

This is my version of a split personality.

At last, I finished the guide. I returned to the book. Theoretically. In fact, I still had another impediment: I vastly preferred working on my LGBT humor blog, posting funny photos and cartoons and writing brief posts. The book wasn't getting short shrift; it was getting no shrift.

One day I asked Anne, "Do you think I should stop the blog altogether and just work on the book?"

"I've been waiting for you to ask me that," she said, before giving me an answer that amounted to #%&@ yes!

So I'm back at it, and only it. Unless I can find another distraction. Perhaps a party for our first anniversary . . .

Chapter 16

Round about the time I backed away from this book, the new DSM-5 came out. Its debut earned the front page of *The Seattle Times*. I marked hoarding disorder officially becoming its own diagnosis in the most appropriate way: I hoarded the *Times*.

Chapter 17

Now back to the concrete examples of a life stuck in concrete.

I've discussed how The Evil One prevails at home. He turns experiences like taking out the trash and doing the laundry into his personal festivals.

Now let's you, Fred and I leave the house, get in the car and run some errands. I need to stop at the library to return a book. What could be simpler than parking behind the library and tossing a book into the book drop?

Surgery could be simpler.

As I pull into a parking spot, my nerves start to tingle. I get out of the car, book in hand, and the tingling increases. I know what Fred requires of me. Walking toward the book drop, I flip through the book several times to check that nothing is in the pages that shouldn't be. Say, a bill, or a credit card, or a . . . Rolls-Royce.

I open the metal flap, insert the book and close the flap. I still fear there's something in the book. Sometimes the fear is low and I can move on, physically and mentally. When it's high, I have to force my legs to walk away from the book drop as my mind swirls with a near conviction that I've just lost something important.

I sit in the car, unable to move on to the next errand until I've put this one to rest. In an effort to convince myself that nothing extraneous hid amidst the pages, I try to re-create what I saw when flipping through them.

Talk about a waste of energy. I'm performing the first compulsion over again, this time without the prop.

Whether the anxiety has lowered or not, eventually I need to leave. After all, I have other errands to sweat over.

At the post office I stand in line, concentrating on the task of buying stamps. If I plan to use cash, I open my wallet to check that the cash is there. When it's my turn at the counter I show impressive dexterity, half my brain making small talk with the postal clerk while the other half follows all the details of the transfer.

Then the real work begins. The checkapalooza.

Clutching everything, I walk over to an empty area of the post office. I pore over the receipt the clerk gave me, checking how much the stamps cost, how much money I gave the clerk and how much change I should've received. I count the change, and make sure to put it into my wallet. If I paid with a debit card, I carefully place the card back in its proper slot in my wallet.

If Fred remains unconvinced that all is well, I'll check everything again in the car. That Mazda Protégé has seen more checking than the boards of the Montreal Forum.

Lastly—or, at last—I pull into the grocery store to pick up a few items. Naturally I eyeball a sale price more than once to make sure I read it correctly. I review my grocery list now and then so I don't forget anything. At the checkout I again chat with the clerk while being careful to swipe my debit card properly and push the right buttons.

The market is usually too congested for me to do my checking immediately after paying for the groceries. Other customers selfishly want to leave the store rather than stack up behind me as I scrutinize my receipt.

So it's back to the driver's seat to review the evidence. What was the grand total? Did I get the advertised sale price on the avocados? Did she give me the right change? Is all that change now in my wallet?

The best possible outcome is that after going over the receipt just once, I get the "click." That's when I know something is true; if there's doubt, it's minimal doubt. I'm not sure why I began calling it that. Maybe because the information clicks into place. At any rate, I live for the click, because it's so flipping rare.

What I usually experience after looking over the receipt is a heaping helping of doubt. So I check again, and again and again, trying to make the doubt go away, trying to be sure.

Welcome to the OCD doom loop. The world's worst thrill ride.

Perversely, the more I check, the less likely I am to achieve the certainty I want. Eventually I'm worn out, frustrated and my mind feels like rice pudding.

When I reach that stage, I'm thoroughly uninclined to do any other errands. In other words, I surrender.

I drive home and put my purchases away. Then I review all the errands in my head: "Supposed to return book—put in drop—post office—bought stamps—they're upstairs—receipt here--wallet there—bought groceries—put away—receipt here—card in wallet—keys there."

Once I'm convinced of the accuracy of my inarticulate checklist, I, receipts in hand, make for my checkbook to enter all the financial transactions in the register. If I delay, I fear there's a greater chance of making a financial error. I think I actually fear that the figures on the receipts will somehow change.

After I take care of that part, I put the receipts into the checking account folder in my file cabinet. Then I look at my day planner to see that all the errands I just did are written on today's page. If one is missing, that's an uh-oh. Not only do I have to hurriedly write it in to make the page accurate, that's just the excuse Fred needs to require another round of checklist reviewing.

Finally, I'm done. Unless Fred prompts more checking.

For me, there's no such thing as a quick errand.

I check when I'm in, I check when I'm out, Fred does the Hokey Pokey and he shakes me all about.

Chapter 18

Many moons ago I decided to be a journalist. I wanted to tell people's stories. I didn't know I'd end up telling my own.

When I chose this career, Fred must've licked his lips and said, "This'll be fun."

Since I finished a Master's degree in nonfiction writing in 1989 and began working as a freelance writer, I've written news stories, feature stories, travel stories, op-ed pieces and, for about a decade, a biweekly humor column. The type of writing makes little difference; Fred is always there, doing his part to make the process an agony.

Consider his impact on an essential facet of journalism, quoting people. When I interview a source for a story, I write down what she says. Or do I? In that moment I can be seized with doubt that I accurately wrote down in my notebook the words she just finished saying.

I developed a bizarre habit to compensate. I repeat what she said, and then add, "Hmm, that's interesting," and pause. I'm waiting for her to respond, "That's not what I said. I said x, y and z."

In this way, I'm dragging the interviewee into my checking. I'm sharing the wealth.

I've never used a tape recorder, which you might think would remove any need to check. It wouldn't. When I got to the writing, I'd have to listen over and over to the tape to assure myself that I was transcribing it correctly.

Sometimes a person says something so useful and I want to get the quote so badly that the anxiety pushes it right out of my brain. Those are the worst moments of all. That's why I should move to a tape recorder. Losing great quotes for no reason makes me want to take my brain out of my head and run it through a carwash.

Later, trying to write the story, I have fresh spasms of doubt over quotes. It might be a week after the interview, and I might've forgotten everything else about it, but when I reach the quotes I stewed over during the interview, I stew anew.

Then, since Fred has me doubting the quotes' accuracy, I question whether I can even use them. Sometimes, out of this abject fear of getting something wrong, I don't use them. That makes for a weaker story. Along with a heap of self-loathing and a frustration headache in the moment.

Of course, I also worry profusely over facts. During the interview I might double-check with the subject the spelling of his name or his date of birth, or triple-check the depth of his loathing for the Cleveland Browns. I remember taking notes for a travel story on a Las Vegas hotel and standing in the atrium for an hour, debating with myself whether my notes truly captured the tropical, leafy scene. Doubtless security at the newly opened Mirage wondered if I was ever going to move on. So did I.

But Fred gets particularly souped up later, while I'm writing. After typing in a fact gleaned during the interview from my notebook, I stare at the screen, then back at my notebook, then back at the screen, back and forth, back and forth, waiting to be convinced that I reproduced the fact accurately.

Sometimes I get the click. Sometimes I don't, and have to carry on writing the story, even though I believe there's a strong chance I've just manufactured a whopper.

Aiding and abetting Fred during this process is the fact that I have God-awful handwriting, and can be seized with the fear that I'm mis-reading a word. Maybe he said he cooks with scallions, but I'm reading it as stallions. An emotional tug-of-war ensues.

My scribbling is yet another reason to use a tape recorder, or digital voice recorder or whatever well-functioning journalists use these days. But if I know me—or if I know Fred—in no time at all I'd be doubting that I'm hearing the words correctly. How many times can you replay a tape before it starts to smolder?

I use and abuse Google to check, say, on a date in history, or which words in a book title are capitalized. When I discover more than one answer to my question, I'm torn: That's bad because I could choose the wrong answer, or that's good because I'm not the only one who'll be wrong.

That's as close as I get to flexibility.

In addition to sweating over whether my quotes and facts are right and whether I reproduced them perfectly, I also cringe over whether I'm interpreting them correctly. This quote sounds like he meant this, but what if he didn't?

I'll reveal myself to be the worst journalist since Ted Baxter.

On occasion I contact a source during the writing process to double-check a fact or an interpretation. This isn't an unusual step to take in the journalism world, and the source might see it as positive, an indica-tion that I'm a reporter who cares about being accurate.

Brother, you don't know the half of it.

The sportswriter Red Smith famously said, "There's nothing to writing. All you do is sit down at a typewriter and open a vein." (Except that wasn't exactly how he said it, and it could be that others said it first, but I digress, goddamn it.)

Because I care about my writing, I open a vein. Because of Fred, I require a transfusion afterwards.

Chapter 19

Freelance writing is a tough way to make a living for anyone. With Fred weighing me down as well, my writing career has been distinctly un-lucrative. I'd have made more selling a kidney.

Since I can't survive off freelancing, I've almost always had a second or third job at the same time. I've held a slew of part-time, ostensibly low-stress jobs, the theory being that they would allow me the time, energy and mental space to write.

At various points during these decades I stocked shoes at Sears, women's clothes at Macy's and kitchen gadgets at Crate & Barrel. I worked as a library assistant on both coasts. I taught kids to play kickball and adults to write humor. I tested how people like different types of chocolate and tomato sauce. I took care of children, pets and homes.

Along the way I discovered that Fred is definitely not a snob. No matter how menial the work, he's right there pitching in. What a guy.

When I shelved boxes of shoes in the stockroom, I was supposed to stack them in order of size so the salespeople could easily grab the box they needed. So I shelved the boxes according to size. And I checked that I'd done it right. And I checked again. And I walked away still carrying a pebble or a boulder of doubt.

When I had to mark down skirts, I scanned the price tag, crossed out the old price, wrote the new one, then looked back and forth between the tag and the scanner to see that I'd written the correct price. Then, even if the next item on the rack looked to be identical, I'd still have to scan it to make sure. I couldn't just write the same price as the previous tag. That might be WRONG.

At the library, the front desk would get busy, which meant I tried to keep a tally in my head of everything I had to go back and check. As soon as the customers cleared away, I rushed to the computer records of everyone I'd just helped, to assure myself that I'd checked in that book, or logged that fine, or included all the information in that new patron's record. If another patron interrupted me, I'd swear silently, clamp on a smile and remind myself that I needed to go back to check.

Not that I needed reminding.

I checked over and over that the right person was getting the right chocolate during the right round of taste-testing. Add that extra work to shuttling trays of chocolate back and forth and setting up and cleaning up all day, and by 4:30 I was gobbling baking chocolate just to keep going.

With Fred around, there's no such thing as a low-stress job. I'm capable of worrying about any task, no matter how mundane or how often I've done it. Putting all this extra effort into every form of work is not only draining, not only time-consuming, it's maddening—the sky won't fall if I bring the wrong cast iron skillet out to a customer.

You jest, says Fred. It assuredly will fall. Ditto if you put the wrong price on that lemon zester.

An employer who prizes accuracy wins the lottery by hiring me. An employer who wants anything done this year? Not so much.

Now I work 20 hours a week at a job that feels more worthwhile than my average. At Kaleidoscope Services (KS), we help seniors and disabled folks with their financial and medical needs. I work mainly in the office, answering the phone, creating invoices and banking our deposits.

When I arrive at 8:00 in the morning, I listen to the messages on the voicemail. Then I'm likely to listen again, out of fear that I misheard the phone number, or transposed numbers as I wrote them. Fred likes to get an early start.

Over the next four hours he's my invisible but ever-present companion. He's always lively when I prepare a deposit, a process involving many steps. Fred can get tangled in any of them, but he's particularly aggravating when I'm trying to record in QuickBooks whether a client's payment is for services only, or for services plus reimbursements.

I so fear being inaccurate that when a client's check is just for services I have a devil of a time convincing myself that's true. I look at the client's invoice on the computer, repeatedly peer at the "0" in the reimbursement line and say "No reimbursements" to myself. But in the half-second it takes to get from there back to QuickBooks, Fred plants enough doubt in me that I must return to the invoice and check again.

I'm fertile soil. I sprout doubt faster than kudzu can cover a southerner.

The next day, shortly after I arrive at work, I'm supposed to perform such an easy task, namely tape the bank receipt for that deposit to a photocopy of it. I look at the amount on the receipt. I look at the amount on the photocopy. They're the same. No they're not. I look again. Yes. No. I try to convince myself by saying the figures aloud. I try to convince myself by comparing the numbers one digit at a time.

It's 8:15 and I'm ready to call it a day.

Chapter 20

I haven't written a word of this book in months. Maybe a year—I've lost track. I fell into Fred's embrace and didn't have the wherewithal to knee him in the crotch.

One thing legitimately got in the way. Ten months ago my mother suffered a stroke. I've flown across the country several times to see her and address her care as she went from hospital to rehab facility to nursing home to back to her own house. Long ago Mom named me her Power of Attorney, so I've devoted a good bit of my time to paying her bills, struggling with her insurance company and overseeing her care.

If Mom had grasped the severity of my OCD, she would've sooner named a hydrangea as her POA.

It's been such a struggle, suddenly handling her accounts and being responsible for things I've never dealt with before, like long-term care insurance. Along with the usual Fred-induced checking, I feel the childhood burden that failing my mother is unacceptable. I feel the anxiety in every part of my body. I forget to breathe, which is spectacularly unhelpful.

On the upside, working for a company that helps seniors has shown me that it's impossible to serve perfectly as POA. Inevitable bureaucratic morasses suck everyone in, Fred or no Fred.

This book never left my mind. I believed I'd get back to it soon, despite being so busy taking care of my mother's affairs, working at my job, performing domestic duties, blogging, trying to purge. I believed the book was around the corner, as soon as I finished going through these boxes of papers to make my office more pleasant . . .

I believe in fantasies. I throw up impediments. I'm 53 years old and still Fred's fool.

Of course the fear that the book won't be perfect also shone brightly. Last weekend Anne and I had an argument during which she confessed she's afraid to ask about the book for fear I'll get mad, and I confessed I'm scared to death to start again for fear I'll make mistakes. Not working on it all this time had heightened that fear. If that's even possible.

I promised Anne I'd take a day off from work and jumpstart this book. I'm baaaaack. You didn't know I was gooooone.

Oh, one other thing. I've been grappling with this book for nigh on to four years. I don't have a clue when I'll finish. When I finally do, the statistics and factoids I've offered might be out-of-date. How about you and I make a deal? If you promise not to hold that against me, I promise to see this project through.

Wow. It's common for OCD sufferers to seek reassurance from friends and family. But I've never heard of someone asking it of future readers. Maybe Fred and I have broken new ground. Yup, we're regular trailblazers.

Chapter 21

If someone asks me when my OCD began, I offer a definitive answer: I have no idea.

I do know I was an anxious child. During my elementary school years I wet the bed with alarming regularity; that's a pun, because my parents, at their wits' end, bought a contraption that set off an alarm whenever I peed in my bed. That beast made me even more nervous, and was none too restful for my sister, who occupied the bottom bunk.

In junior high I experienced pronounced social anxiety. Once I worried myself into a monster headache that I used to get out of a sleepover with friends because the prospect terrified me. Either I feared I'd relapse wetting the bed, or I feared making any kind of social faux pas.

Were these early indicators that Fred was ahead? Big ol' blinking signs that I had an anxiety disorder or two to look forward to?

Or was I simply an anxious kid because I was the firstborn endowed with many expectations, or because I grew up in two Ivy League towns, where the pressure to succeed muscles out fluoride as the main substance in the water?

I had other reasons for being anxious. In my house, neither of my parents expressed love verbally or physically. I know now they loved me, but I didn't know it then, so my world didn't feel too stable. I lacked that sense of security, that peace, that comes from knowing you're always loved, even if you flunk a class, crash the car or take pinking shears to your brother's hair.

Deep down, I felt I could justify my existence only by achieving, so I did, in academics, sports, extracurricular activities. Which may have irritated my sister even more than the bed-wetting.

What also did a number on me was my mother's inability to admit making mistakes. When she made one, she either contrived an excuse or pretended the mistake never happened. From her example I learned early that mistakes were unacceptable. I learned that perfection was not only possible, it was required.

It's hard to believe there isn't a direct connection between this childhood instruction in perfection and my adult terror of making mistakes. But who knows? Perhaps Fred was a virgin birth.

Mom is German. Big surprise. No, not all Germans are perfectionists, but Mom has a streak of it wider than the Rhine. There's some sort of safety in it for her, and as a child of war, she has ample reason to aim for safety.

All I know for sure is on a few occasions when I was about 10, after feeling I'd made an egregious mistake or come up short in some way in front of her, I held a knife to my chest, too frightened to do anything with it, but wishing I could so I could stop feeling so badly about myself.

I suspect by 12 all the serotonin in my brain had vacated the premises.

Another source of anxiety was one of which I have no memories. A compelling amount of circumstantial evidence indicates I suffered early sexual abuse.

In my late 20s I underwent hypnosis, because as likely as it seemed that I'd been abused, without memories I couldn't be certain, and I didn't want to accuse anyone falsely. You don't need to have Fred to yearn to get that right. But it helps.

The hypnosis confirmed that I'd been sexually abused and by the person I suspected. However, recently my OCD therapist told me hypnosis is no longer considered reliable, and since I so fear making a mistake, I can't say with total certainty that it happened. I can say much evidence suggests it did. If it did, well, sexual abuse tends to make a child a wee bit tense.

Do I have OCD because my early life was anxious or was my early life anxious because I had OCD? Did I develop a chemical imbalance or was I born with it?

I don't bloody well know. Only Fred knows, and he ain't talking.

Chapter 22

A word about savaging your parents in a memoir.

I hate the idea of pouncing on either of my parents. Why? I love them. In my mother's case, I also early on instinctively became her protector, and now I'm taking on what looks a helluva lot like the opposite role.

Furthermore, blaming the mother is cliched, too easy and chaps my feminist hide.

But having undergone ample therapy for Fred and other matters for decades, I know I can't tell my story and omit my parents, particularly my mother.

I'm trying to provide as complete a picture as I can—like this minion of Fred would do otherwise—so that must include how Mom and I were enmeshed. It's the truth, and I believe I've mentioned my fondness for accuracy. Once or twice.

I have enough distance now to be able to see the reality of our relationship. I'm still fallible—yes, Fred, it's tragic but true—and not
immune from hurts coloring my view, but I strive to be clear-eyed.

I also have enough distance to grasp probable reasons for why she is
the person she is. Born in an industrial region of Germany in 1935, she
was four when Hitler invaded Poland, 10 when the war ended. Along
the way her father and brothers were drafted, wounded, captured. She
was bombed out of her apartment building. She saw untold numbers of
mangled dead bodies. She starved. Her early life was the definition of
instability, and if she sought later to control her world, I get it.

What's that? Am I looking for excuses for her? Stop being so
perceptive.

I want to understand why my mother parented me as she did, not
least so I can explain it away. I know she didn't consciously put excessive and unrelenting pressure on me—after all, that would mean she
made a mistake—but she groomed me for Fred. I want to understand,
I want to forgive and I'm on target to do that by the time I'm 106.

When she could still walk, Mom would stride firmly straight ahead,
often with her head down. You're likely to get somewhere that way, but
you're also likely to run into people. She moved purposefully through
life, meeting all the practical demands of her family and her professional life and her volunteer work in exemplary fashion, but with little
interest in detouring into extraneous areas like self-awareness. I tried
for years to get her to go to therapy, and when she finally did she lasted
as long as it takes to say "This better be covered by insurance."

Mom knows she carries one burden in abundance, German guilt
for the Holocaust. But she doesn't know that she also feels a sort of
guilt when she enjoys herself, that she's most comfortable when she can
complain about how much work she has to do. My enormous capacity
for guilt comes from her, truly the gift that keeps on giving.

When my parents married she was 26 and he was 55, which guaranteed me a lifetime of watching people's jaws drop when I said my folks had 30 years between them.

Or 29 years and two weeks, as my mother prefers to say. I'm not the only one who likes precision.

Dad was 56 when I was born, and my sister and brother followed. He already had a daughter and a son from a previous marriage. In fact, he had two previous marriages, but he didn't count the first one because it was annulled. Dad wasn't tethered to precision.

His age and gender allowed him some parenting distance. Dad was involved—attending my various sporting events, for instance—but not terribly tuned in to who any of us in the family really were. Our personal likes and dislikes were largely unknown to him. As I got older it occurred to me that the characters he created in his novels and plays might be more real to Dad than we were.

Certainly he gave no hint that he recognized the pressure I felt. If I'd had the awareness and bravery to ask him to talk about it with Mom, he'd have agreed, but been out of his emotional depth. It would've been like sending in the team manager to play quarterback.

On his deathbed Dad applied some pressure of his own. "Keep writing," he told me. That was in 1998, and he had no idea what Fred was doing to my writing. Had he known, I think he would've said something less demanding, like "Keep breathing."

We shared the writing bond, and I think with those words he was bestowing a kind of blessing. We shared a number of other things, ranging from sports to humor, and of his five kids I'm the most like him. But I'm also much like my mother, with our mutual interest in politics, travel, history, our deep sense of responsibility and . . . our abhorrence of making mistakes.

I'm a lot of him and a lot of her. It's mighty crowded in here.

Chapter 23

Where was I before I needed to unburden myself of guilt? Oh right, I was explaining that I don't know when my OCD began. Now I get to tell you that the experts don't know why it began. My but we're a clueless bunch.

At this stage, the specific cause of OCD is a mystery. Scientists have picked up bits and pieces of the answer, however, and here are some of them, ripped off liberally from a public presentation given by two psychologists, both of whom I trust, and one of whom I pay a lot of money:

- OCD is a neurobehavioral disorder, which means both biology and learned behavior play roles
- OCD sufferers inherit a genetic vulnerability for Fred-ness
- OCD appears related to a lack of serotonin in specific parts of the brain

- Biology seems to determine who will develop OCD, but learned behavior is essential to maintain the ongoing joy that is the Fred experience
- The "OCD cycle"—you experience a trigger, you obsess, you feel intense anxiety, you perform a compulsion, you feel relief, then you start all over again—is ridiculously hard to break out of because you learn the only way to quell the anxiety is to perform the compulsion

All of this is helpful to know. But it's clear that most things about OCD remain to be discovered. That makes it an exciting time to be studying the disorder.

By contrast, it's never an exciting time to have it.

Chapter 24

Though I was largely unaware of it growing up, I aimed to be perfect. The alternative, being average, meant I might alienate my parents, and that was too scary.

Then a funny thing happened on my way to perfection: honest-to-God failure.

Since elementary school I'd had difficulty with math. I finessed my way through until I hit high school, where I actually flunked introductory algebra and geometry.

Talk about stressful. I couldn't understand the concepts, and I couldn't understand why I couldn't understand. Neither could anyone else. The prevailing theory was that I wasn't trying hard enough.

I hated the prevailing theory.

My parents hired a tutor to come to our house. All that got me was the scintillating experience of being just as embarrassed at home as at school that I couldn't grasp the most basic principles. I was lost in a world of melodramatic mathematics.

So baffled were my parents and teachers that I struggled mightily in one academic area while excelling in all the others that someone suggested I see a psychiatrist. Apparently around 1980 in Hanover, N.H., the default reaction to academic failure was she must be nuts.

I saw the psychiatrist. He proposed I be tested. I was. Holy Archimedes, I had a learning disability.

That was good news, because it meant all this failing wasn't from lack of effort. That was also bad news, because it meant I had a deep flaw, which meant I could never be perfect. Call it a mixed blessing. Or a mixed stressing.

The testing had also revealed my IQ. I can't remember the number, but it was decidedly mediocre, which upset me more than anything else. How was I going to go out and do the great things expected of me lumbered with a so-so IQ? I felt guilty, like I was letting my parents down by having such an IQ.

It never occurred to me to be mad at them for creating me with a mediocre IQ and a learning disability. Nor did I ever question the accuracy of the tests, nor realize that being a mass of nerves while taking them might've impacted the results.

I had tunnel vision. And was on my way to being a train wreck.

Chapter 25

After the Great Math Mystery was solved, I continued to see the psychiatrist at my request. One day my father came into a session and told the shrink that I had the quickest mind of anyone he'd ever known. I was ridiculously proud. His words also helped balance the IQ shock.

Presumably the reason I carried on with the psychiatrist was the relief that came from unloading. I got to vent to him about the parental pressure I felt. I told him how my mother would occasionally do my homework, another way of letting me know that perfection was required. But that I couldn't achieve it by myself. It was darn squishy between that rock and hard place.

I vented too about the teenage social hierarchy. I told him how much it irked me that the way to be popular was to drink or do drugs. I thought that was limited and simple-minded. My poor friends had to hear me expound on the wrongness of the social system—sometimes while we drank or toked. I was a geek-jock who simultaneously loathed and longed for coolness. Not being at the top of the heap made me feel not just lesser, but also that I was letting my parents down.

I sense a theme here, this fear of disappointing them.

My feelings about how people should behave, whether it was a high school junior dropping acid for status or a president joking about blowing up Russia, were fervent. At some point in my teens or 20s, Dad told me that I had an overdeveloped sense of right and wrong.

Now I have to wonder whether I just absorbed this black and white thinking from my mother, who judged people according to a narrow code of conduct, or was this another example of Fred's early onset?

Meaning, dammit, was this scrupulosity, yet another symptom of OCD?

How I loathe Fred with everything that's in me. Yes, he's in me too, but let's not weaken my hatred by splitting hairs.

Since I hadn't put two and two together before now, I asked my present OCD therapist, Travis, whether this early rigidity around personal behavior sounded like scrupulosity to him. He said it usually manifests religiously.

Whereupon I thanked God that I'm not religious.

Travis added it can manifest in a need to confess, and I flashed back to that experience in fifth grade when I held a knife to my chest. The next morning I told my mother that I'd tried to kill myself. And there was the time in high school I confessed to her that my boyfriend and I had gotten more intimate than she suspected.

Scrupulosity? Or just garden-variety enmeshment?

In looking back to find the origins of Fred, I might be assigning him more tentacles than he had. Not a problem. Since he lives to wreak havoc, he's only too happy to take any credit going.

Chapter 26

If scrupulosity isn't part of my Fred, let's put that aside and turn to a different matter altogether. Believe it or not, there's another affliction out there in mental-health land that's called obsessive-compulsive personality disorder.

I bet you didn't know tiptoeing through the psychological tulips was going to be this complicated. If it helps, I didn't either.

Obsessive-compulsive disorder is an anxiety disorder.

Wait, no, it isn't. That updated DSM did indeed remove OCD from the anxiety disorders classification. OCD got its own classification, which made Fred so conceited he wasn't fit to live with.

The obsessive-compulsive disorders include OCD itself, hoarding disorder, body dysmorphic disorder and some other fun-filled sicknesses. The experts decided to separate obsessive-compulsive disorders from anxiety disorders because of a difference in neurochemistry, but Fred believes it's simply a case of his genius finally being recognized.

Let's return to my original point. Obsessive-compulsive disorder (OCD) is one of the obsessive-compulsive disorders, while obsessive-compulsive personality disorder (OCPD) is a personality disorder.

That sentence reads drier than sand. Blame all the DSM shenanigans.

One of my OCD therapists over the last decade suggested my mother might have OCPD, so in trying to sort out for this book what I have and why, I dipped into the DSM-5 for an explanation of OCPD.

I read that OCPD is a "pervasive pattern of preoccupation with orderliness, perfectionism, and mental and interpersonal control, at the expense of flexibility, openness, and efficiency."

My stomach tightened a little.

The person with this disorder is "preoccupied with details, rules, lists, order, organization, or schedules to the extent that the major point of the activity is lost."

My stomach tightened a little more.

The person "shows perfectionism that interferes with task completion (e.g., is unable to complete a project because his or her own overly strict standards are not met)."

You mean like being unable to finish a book?

The person is "excessively devoted to work and productivity to the exclusion of leisure activities."

Anne just complained how I've kept us from vacationing out of duty.

The person is "overconscientious, scrupulous, and inflexible about matters of morality, ethics, or values."

See the previous chapter.

The person is "unable to discard worn-out or worthless objects," is "reluctant to delegate tasks or to work with others unless they submit to exactly his or her way of doing things," shows a "miserly spending style" and displays "rigidity and stubbornness."

I expected to see my mother in the definition of OCPD. I wound up seeing myself. That's just rude.

I don't display all the tendencies listed above, but I'm worried. How many disorders can a person have before she springs a leak?

Again, I put a question to Travis: "Do I strike you as a person with OCPD?"

"Not that I know of," he answered. "It's not something that's jumped out at me."

Hasn't jumped out at him. Good. At least I haven't made like a mental-health jack-in-the-box.

Travis added that I already have the hoarding diagnosis, which is one of the criteria for OCPD. He and I would need to review the other criteria to see if an OCPD diagnosis fits. Also, it can be hard to disentangle OCD and OCPD, since some types of OCD look like OCPD, said Travis.

Y'know, let's skip it. Getting this far into the weeds might be more harmful than helpful. I have a pretty good idea of what my issues are, and so does Travis. And so does Fred.

I'll say this, though: If I do have both OCD and OCPD, I damn well better not get chronic obstructive pulmonary disease down the road. To have OCD, OCPD and COPD is to live in alphabet hell, and I'll never know whether to check or wheeze.

Chapter 27

Remember all my woes with math? I don't blame you if the answer is no—that was three chapters and several psychological concepts ago.

Suffice it to say that despite those math travails, I managed to graduate in the top portion of my high school class. I didn't manage, however, to get into my first choice for college. Bowdoin College wait-listed me, which again made me feel like I'd failed and let my parents down.

I removed myself from the waiting list, knowing that even if I got in I'd be haunted that this lesser acceptance meant I was a lesser person. I went with my second choice, Colby College. I still remember the poster in the senior lounge that listed the schools we'd be attending, and having a sinking feeling when I saw Colby next to my name.

It was a very good school. But I was supposed to go to the best, and our Bible in that Ivy League town, the Barron's book, listed Colby as a notch below the best. Though the learning disability had technically disqualified me from perfection, I still knew greatness was required. In fact, I think I became even more driven, because now I felt I had a major flaw for which I needed to compensate.

I was going to be perfectly imperfect.

God, just writing about it is exhausting.

At any rate, in the fall of 1981 I headed to Waterville, Maine, with a mug, two sets of towels and an entrenched case of perfectionism. In this process of looking back at my early days through the lens of Fred, I realize It's impossible for me to pinpoint where my perfectionism ended and my OCD began. Perfectionism morphed into OCD; OCD is perfectionism without brakes.

Chapter 28

Truth be told, I was petrified of going to college at all, because the years of Mom having dabbled in my German homework or rewritten my history papers had left me supremely doubtful I could do college work myself.

And bringing her along was out of the question.

Freshman year I did well enough with one glaring exception. I damn near flunked biology. My theory is that I mentally lumped math and science together, so all the anxiety I brought to math I also transferred to science. I had piggy-back anxiety.

Sophomore year I took only classes that appealed to me, and I excelled. Because I was interested in so many subjects, from English to history to sociology to film, I chose a major that was wide-ranging.

I majored in American Studies, and minored in Fred.

If I don't know exactly when my OCD took root, I do know when it began to bloom. The condition, along with hoarding, flowered in my later college years. Unbeknownst to me, Fred was coming out like a debutante.

I spent my junior year in the then-West German city of Munich. Partly because I hung around for the most part with other Americans, but mainly, I suspect, because of the life-long stress around learning the language, my German barely improved. I was the anti-poster child for spending a year abroad.

I had fun, though, and naturally when a person lives in another country she collects souvenirs. I kept theater programs, beer coasters, the usual things . . . along with TV listings and junk mail, not the usual things.

That flotsam and jetsam came back to America with me, along with stories I found compelling from *The International Herald Tribune*. The next year, back in Maine, a friend and I shared the cost of a subscription to *The Boston Globe*. She read it. I stored it. Oh, I meant to read it, and still believed I would, as the stacks of newspapers against the wall expanded.

For the next 30 years, stacks of paper remained a constant feature of my interior decorating. I can say with confidence it's not a prize-winning look.

By my early 20s, then, I was a hoarder, and completely unaware of it. All those newspapers just meant that I had plentiful interests, which was true, and I'd get around to reading them eventually, which was mostly untrue.

Sometimes I read a section with scissors in hand, suspecting I'd just need to keep a story or five. I was on my way to developing a personal library that was the envy of . . . nobody.

Chapter 29

I was just as oblivious to something worse that also descended on me around that time. During my senior year of college, when the classes were the most demanding, I couldn't keep up with the required reading. Novels, nonfiction, it didn't matter—I struggled mightily to finish any book.

Since elementary school I'd been a whiz of a reader. I impressed teachers with my vocabulary and speed. I read lavishly for fun.

But by my last semester of college, it was like my brain developed a charley horse.

I read a line, then instead of automatically darting forward to the next line, I went backwards. I reread the line. Sometimes I reread it again. And again.

I was so afraid I'd misunderstood something, or missed a fact, that I reread to be sure. Fred had placed that doubt in me, so I checked and checked again to remove the doubt. I hadn't even heard of OCD at this point, but clearly it had heard of me.

The need to read backward like this came on me slowly, part of the reason I didn't realize what was happening. It seemed nothing but logical, as I chased good grades, that I needed to be sure about what I read. And American Studies majors face so much reading—surely I was overloaded? I didn't grasp the reality, that my reading speed had gone from galloping to galumphing.

The result was I walked into my senior seminar with the week's book unfinished, maybe not even begun. I felt guilty, of course, and petrified that I'd be called on. If the professor asked me about the white working class in the 60s and I answered, "They were white and they worked. In the 60s," he might catch on that I hadn't read the material.

There was little chance I'd speak of my own accord—I hardly talked in class. In high school and college, owing to that paralyzing mix of shyness and fear of making a mistake, I rarely opened my trap. I knew the cliche about learning from mistakes, but since all I felt when I made one was shame, I preferred to avoid them altogether and do without their educational properties.

Looking back, I can see that it was during those college years that I started to lose out on life. Fred's needs began to trump mine. As a simple example, I wanted to walk in the college's arboretum during my senior year, relax in nature. But I never did, even though it was within a pine cone's throw of my dorm, out of the fear that I couldn't afford the time.

After all, I had newspapers to cut up and books to read backwards.

It's clear to me 30 years later that if procrastination is the thief of time, OCD is time's mugger.

Chapter 30

Despite these manifestations of Fred kicking in, and despite misfires with panic-inducing science classes I had to take due to distribution requirements, I managed to graduate respectably, finishing cum laude and, most satisfying to me, winning the American Studies Prize for having the highest GPA in the major.

Fred had caught me, but he didn't yet have me hook, line and stinker.

Following graduation I moved in with my boyfriend of a few years. Alex was six years older than I, had visited me often in Maine when he wasn't at home in Manhattan or on the road as a magazine writer. Now that I'd finished school, it was time to cohabitate.

And time to choose a career, or at least a path. As a college senior and after, I narrowed my interests down to publishing, museum work, journalism and even becoming an American Studies professor.

I decided against the latter, because I didn't want to live an ivory-tower life. Now I know that I wouldn't have lasted six months in a graduate program. My unknown-to-me reading challenge, that new and pronounced slowness, would've collided head-on against colossal reading lists. I would've had to choose between not finishing the books, or getting six minutes of sleep every night.

Either could've led to an ugly scene with me hurling the collected works of Sinclair Lewis from a bell tower at 3 a.m.

I suspect now that, if I'd followed the academic path, exhaustion and frustration would've led me to a breakdown, and I'd have been forced to become aware of Fred sooner than I did. Of course, OCD wasn't well-known then, and I might've been misdiagnosed as having attention deficit disorder. Or schizophrenia. Or an allergy to writers from Minnesota.

As it happened, a friend interning at the PBS show then called "The MacNeil/Lehrer NewsHour" alerted me to an opening for a PR intern. It wasn't actual journalism, but I leaped at the chance to work for such a prominent program.

Most of my tasks, like giving tours to international journalists and schlepping interview transcripts to print outlets, I handled well. A couple of tasks I didn't handle well enough.

"The NewsHour" paid a company to transcribe shows, and I was required, as I recall, to fact-check the preliminary version and send it back. Eventually the company complained to my boss that I wasn't turning the work around with sufficient speed.

I recall that part right enough. Fred rarely lets me forget a mistake. He's probably stitched them all on a series of samplers.

What I had to fact-check wasn't arduous for the most part, so chances are I just wouldn't let the stuff out of my clutches till I was certain it was accurate. I can't imagine I would've fudged it and hoped for the best like any other 22-year-old intern making $50 a week would've done.

The other likely explanation is that I was too busy taking too long on other tasks, especially the one where I had to organize print transcripts going back years in giant file cabinets.   What I remember of that endeavor is that I spent so much time getting it right that I had to appeal for help.   Some part of me knew I shouldn't require it, that the job shouldn't take this long, and I was embarrassed.

Fred, on the other hand, swelled with pride.

Chapter 31

As part of organizing those print transcripts, I needed to cull them. I did—right into my personal collection.

Transcripts of shows on, say, Geraldine Ferraro, punk music or the L.A. Olympics went home with me. Leave compelling information in the trash? Not gonna happen. Actually reading the information wouldn't happen either, but I was a long way from figuring that out.

I walked those transcripts across Manhattan and added them to my paper stash. Alex dubbed the stash my "archives," a wonderfully benign and respectable designation. Throughout our relationship, when he was on the road writing for *Sports Illustrated*, he mailed me envelopes of newspaper and magazine articles he knew would appeal to me. With him being gone so often, it was a way of staying connected.

While Alex connected, Fred invaded. I was involved with two men and didn't know it.

Sometimes I read the articles Alex sent and then threw them out. Sometimes I read them and saved them in the archives. Sometimes I didn't read them and saved them in the archives.

The bottom line: I saved a lot of articles. I was the potentate of paper.

Because he worked for a Time-Life publication, Alex regularly received all the company magazines for free. He didn't always bring home copies of *Time* and *People* and others, thank goodness, but those publications crossed paths with me often enough. By now, you can guess what happened when they did: a scissor-fest hootenanny.

Chapter 32

Perversely, the more interested I was in a magazine, the less likely I was to read it. If Alex came home with an issue of *Life* all about old Hollywood, one of my favorite topics, I would look at the cover gleefully—and put the magazine right down. Without knowing it, I was afraid I wouldn't read the issue accurately, or wouldn't retain what I read. My gut as much as told me, "Back away from the magazine and nobody gets hurt."

I understood my gut's silent direction that I was to read it later, when I could give it proper attention. Which would be when the Statue of Liberty came in to pinch hit at Yankee Stadium.

Only through writing this book do I now realize how long that need for Nirvana-like conditions has been with me, and in how many areas. Today, when I delay opening my mail until I feel like I can handle it, or decline to write until conditions are perfect, that's Fred shifting me out of gear into neutral, just as he did three decades ago.

And it now appears to me that underpinning every one of these examples of avoidance is the fear of making a mistake. I might mis-remember what I read; I might separate a bill from its return envelope; I might write a factual error into a column.

You've heard of paralysis by analysis? Welcome to terror of error.

This business of wanting to read a magazine story, but being unable to in the moment because of OCD-instilled fear, and then hoarding the magazine instead, is why I'll always think of my OCD and my hoarding as being connected, despite experts decreeing they're separate afflictions.

My first Fred (OCD) and second Fred (hoarding) have a symbiotic relationship. I can't read a magazine because of first Fred, and that contributes, literally, to second Fred. Think of my OCD as a shark, and my hoarding as a suckerfish attached to it, benefitting from it.

And think of me as fish food.

Chapter 33

On the subject of OCD-instilled fear, I recall one set of circumstances where I escaped Fred. I'd be reading a book on a plane, and be repeatedly re-reading to check that I absorbed a sentence correctly. Then I'd look over Alex's shoulder and start scanning the newspaper he was reading, and suddenly I could read like I used to. Quickly, with total comprehension, and no checking.

I wasn't really reading the newspaper, right? Just glancing at it for a second. I faked Fred out. But when I returned to my book, I was back in quicksand. Ditto if I took the paper from Alex.

My choices at the time were to continue my anguished form of reading, or to superglue Alex to my side so I could read over his shoulder for the rest of my life.

Chapter 34

Ultimately I decided that I wanted a career of writing for newspapers or magazines, so I enrolled in the University of New Hampshire's Master's program in nonfiction writing.

Fred enrolled as well. For all I know, he may've gotten a scholarship.

Having no formal training in journalism, I started with the basic classes in writing news and feature stories. I soon adopted the habit, after conducting an interview, of settling in an empty classroom for the purpose of poring over my reporter's notebook, checking that I could read what I wrote, that the quotes made sense, that it was clear who said what.

It didn't matter if the story was a class assignment, or for the student newspaper or a professional outlet. Everything required checking. If I couldn't assure myself that this really was what the person said, I'd just keep reaching for certainty with more checking. If I couldn't achieve certainty, I'd agonize over the chance, nay likelihood, that I'd messed up.

Fred really dug grad school.

One of the reasons I chose UNH was the option of taking classes in other kinds of writing and in literature. In my second year I took a lit class for which I had to write a paper of publishable quality on anarchist Emma Goldman's autobiography.

I read the two volumes at the speed of extremely slow light. I slogged. I suffered. I noticed the oils on my hand were coloring the pages, but I didn't notice that reading shouldn't be like this. I just thought I so wanted to understand everything properly, and that was absolutely true.

I wrote the paper without finishing the second volume. Were she alive, Emma Goldman would've roundly scolded me in several languages.

She wouldn't have needed to, since I felt ample shame all by myself. But I still didn't realize I was now reading as slowly as I must've when I first made the acquaintance of that non-anarchist duo, Dick and Jane.

If I didn't recognize the crawl at which I now read, I certainly didn't realize why—that Fred had instilled the fear in me that I was misunderstanding nearly every sentence I read.

Over two years at UNH I learned about everything from ledes to New Journalism to how to pitch a story to an editor. But I didn't learn I'd become Fred's favorite toy.

In the spring of 1989 Fred and I graduated with M.A. degrees. Mine was a Master of Arts; his was a Master of Aggravation.

Chapter 35

I'd begun freelance writing at UNH, and Alex planned to take a hiatus from *Sports Illustrated* to work on a book, so we decided to live together in picturesque Portsmouth, N.H., and write.

Alex has always been a disciplined writing machine, writing faster than I can speak. In concert with a co-author, he churned out chapters for his book on cheating in college basketball that would become a bestseller. I reviewed every chapter for clarity and flow, but there usually wasn't much with which to quibble. The man was even an accomplished typist, for God's sake.

I talked to a college friend on the phone during this period who asked if it was hard for me to be with someone who was such a writing success when I was just starting out. I said the gap between us was so great that it seemed ludicrous to fret over it.

It helped that Alex had a generous spirit and was in no way belittling. I also assumed I'd eventually reach his lofty heights. I expected that of myself, and I knew everyone around me expected it.

Fred couldn't have found a bigger patsy if he tried.

I earnestly endeavored to sell freelance pieces in the way it was done before the internet took hold, by pitching ideas to magazine editors over the phone and mailing travel stories to newspapers. As I critiqued Alex's work, he critiqued mine.

One November day when Alex was out of town, I sat down at my desk aiming to incorporate his edits on what was probably a travel piece. With the hard copy on which he'd written placed to the right of my computer, and starting at the beginning of the story, I set about doing something I'd done many times before.

That day I was particularly plodding, slowly deciding yes or no on his suggestions, and even more slowly executing them. Certainty about whether a change altered the meaning or accuracy played as hard to get as the Loch Ness monster.

About halfway through the story I looked at his notes, and back at my sentence on the screen, back again at his notes, and back again at my sentence, back and forth, back and forth. I couldn't understand what he meant. I couldn't understand my sentence. I couldn't understand anything. I kept trying, willing my brain to unscramble.

Finally, I couldn't understand why I'd want to live.

I'd had the experience before of checking so often I landed in this mental purgatory where nothing makes sense, but never so intense or long-lasting, never with such a robust sense of hopelessness. All those experiences had been leading to this one.

With Alex away, I'd reached the abyss alone. I told myself I had two choices: kill myself or get into therapy.

Clearly I wasn't in the mood for multiple options.

I paced. I wrestled internally with myself. What was the point of going on if my brain was mush? It was the most important part of me, and it was failing. That left nothing. I was nothing.

Against that cheery backdrop, I decided I really had no choice but to live, owing to an external factor. My older half-brother had committed suicide six years before. He'd suffered from bipolar disorder, then called manic depression, which we hadn't known. I couldn't force my family to grapple with another suicide. I just couldn't.

I might be nothing, but at least I'd be a living nothing.

Chapter 36

I chose a therapist out of the phonebook, made an appointment and began the process of trying to figure out why my mind had turned into an Edsel.

The more she got to know me, the more the therapist, Carol, could ask relevant questions. Had my brain seized up while trying to incorporate Alex's changes because he was a prominent journalist and I felt lesser? Was the experience a variation on Mom doing my homework and I lost confidence?

Had a pixie heisted my cerebrum?

Over the next few years, in individual and group sessions, Carol and I tackled everything. I undertook a conscious individuating from my mother, which was just as much fun as it sounds, but above all I worked on The Big Three. Had I been sexually abused as a child? What was my sexual orientation? And did I have this condition, that I don't think I'd even heard of before, called obsessive-compulsive disorder?

The answers I settled on were very likely; bisexual; and God damn it, probably.

Oddly, even as a raging incidence of Fred caused me to go into therapy, it was the OCD question that took the longest to be answered. Even odder when you consider that Carol had it too. But her OCD manifested differently—she feared that she'd run over someone while driving, and would have to go back again and check—and maybe we didn't make the connection, or maybe in the early 90s too little was still known.

Or maybe I just rebelled at the idea of having such a failing. If I could barely deal with having a learning disability, a mental illness was as welcome as leprosy.

Carol dispatched me to a local psychiatrist to discuss anti-depressants, which I resisted taking because it seemed weak. I remember talking about OCD with the shrink, and explaining the pressure to be perfect, and her responding that as far as she knew that wouldn't cause OCD, that it was a brain chemistry issue. I felt in that moment a profound sense that the lifelong pressure was indeed a factor, but what did I know? I was a new and distinctly unwilling entrant into the world of crazy.

Presumably it was she who sent me to the OCD Clinic at Massachusetts General Hospital in Boston for the final word on whether I had this condition or not. I'd like to provide a fulsome description of the testing process, and who had the honor of bestowing the diagnosis upon me and how I felt when I heard those words. But I remember nothing. Bupkis. Some part of me just blocked all that out.

I can't believe this was Fred's doing—he'd prefer I remember every painful minute. He'd even be up for a little anniversary party each year.

All I remember is driving home from Boston the day it became official and feeling like a medicine ball had moved into my stomach.

My guilt and anguish for being defective filled up the VW Golf like a dangling 7-Eleven air freshener.

I still couldn't wholly accept the idea that there was something so wrong with me. That denial ebbed and flowed over time. I think it finally disappeared. Yesterday.

Chapter 37

There are moments I look back on, painful and baffling at the time, that couldn't be clearer now. Like when, during graduate school, I found myself unable to throw out some unimportant piece of paper. I became so aggravated that I marched over to the metal sink in my apartment and set the paper on fire, just to get rid of it. Instead of relief, I felt regret. I still wanted to have kept it.

And there was that time I sat on my apartment floor in Portsmouth, readying a manuscript for mailing. I had the story, the accompanying letter to the editor and a return envelope to insert into a manila envelope. I checked everything repeatedly, of course. I looked at the letter I'd signed, and wound up getting stuck on whether my name really was Leslie Robinson.

I couldn't convince myself of my own name.

If ever I'd wanted a different name, that was my chance.

It wasn't amnesia, it was Fred. Caught in such an anxiety tempest, I doubtless tried to mollify myself by vowing to be more careful going forward—meaning check more.

One of the many tricky things about having OCD is sorting out which behaviors are caused by the illness, and which are just your own idiosyncrasies. I remember, when Alex and I lived together in Portsmouth, walking to the post office to mail my manuscripts, but declining Alex's request to take his mail along as well. It wasn't rudeness or self-absorption or revenge for a tiff or generic personal weirdness. It was Fred, the fear that if I divided my attention between two tasks, something would go wrong with the first.

Try explaining that when you don't understand it yourself. I promised to take his mail later that day, but I must've sounded flakier than an apple strudel.

Then there was the matter of my not reading Alex's stories in *Sports Illustrated*, which also understandably annoyed him. I'm sure I meant to—as soon as I had the time to read them perfectly. So, never.

When I began reading picture books in bed, I told Alex that I'd become interested in writing them. That was true, but there was another truth: Picture books didn't plague me with the need to check, like any book meant for someone eight years of age or older did. And if a yearning to check arose, well, picture books have few pages and big print, so checking was downright speedy. We must've been quite a sight before turning off the lights, Alex reading a historical tome on the Mississippi Delta, while I hunkered down with "Make Way for Ducklings."

As I began to get therapy specifically for OCD, a few things did become clear, and I explained what I could to my partner. If he found me staring into space when we were due to go out, he knew, now, that I was mentally checking, and that I wouldn't leave the apartment till I was satisfied I'd done whatever it was. He waited.

When Alex and I split, one of the hardest parts for me was giving up a person with that kind of patience. Though now he might be accused of enabling me, at the time this felt like white-knight stuff.

But split we did, and it was all to the good, as within a year I realized I wasn't bisexual but lesbian. The only man for me was Fred.

Chapter 38

On a spring day in 1994 in Portsmouth I watched, scared and deeply sad, as Alex drove away in his loaded rental car. The relationship that had begun when I was 18 was over. I was 30 years old, and alone.

Well, not entirely.

If only I'd tied Fred to the roof, Alex could've dumped him in Long Island Sound on his way to the city.

Over the next months, propped up by financial assistance from Alex that he was under no legal obligation to provide, I embarked on my wobbly future. I continued freelance writing. I snagged part-time work with Macy's, where I folded a mean sweater. At the suggestion of Carol the therapist, I started attending the local lesbian group. And I continued to work with Carol, and expanded my trips to Boston to see a psychiatrist and a psychologist at Mass General's OCD clinic.

But I didn't understand the enormity of what having Fred meant.

What I did understand was that there were a number of medications on offer at Mass General. Since I'd gone ahead and tried Prozac—my gateway drug—I was agreeable to trying other meds the shrink suggested. More than agreeable. Now that I had this awful diagnosis, and since she told me some sufferers' symptoms were relieved by taking various antidepressants, I was now hot to try anything that might wipe away my OCD. Anything that might fix me. Anything that might dropkick this hunk of imperfection with which I was now officially burdened.

Which is why my attitude toward pharmaceuticals had gone from no way to hand it over.

I tried antidepressants like Paxil and Zoloft, but they had little impact on my symptoms and produced side effects. The psychiatrist told me a drug that had been successful in Europe would soon be approved in this country, and I proceeded to invest an inordinate amount of hope in Luvox. But after finally getting my mitts on it, I reported, all dejection, that my need to check hadn't abated.

Better living through chemistry my eye.

Chapter 39

As I pined for a drug to rid me of Fred, I worked with the psychologist.

If only I could remember what form the work took. I remember the psychologist, but I can't recall how she and I tackled my need to check. I remember the broad outlines of fighting hoarding, which was at the time considered part of my OCD, a point you might recall since you have a better memory than I do.

Which doesn't appear to be saying a lot.

I know I reported to the psychologist how much paper I'd parted with since our previous appointment. I have an overall sense that I wasn't totally honest with her. Maybe I claimed to have tossed a whole grocery bag of newspaper and hadn't, but promised myself I would later so it would be true. And then couldn't do it.

I didn't consciously lie. It was part wishful thinking and part a lack of understanding of the severity of the problem. I fooled her because I fooled me.

At that time, I just couldn't accept that slips of paper were stronger than I was.

At this time, I'm embarrassed at the insufficiency of my memory. But then I, yes, remember that this has long been an issue for me. I remember almost nothing prior to kindergarten. I know that for my entire young life arguing with my mother made me so anxious that I'd dissociate, be unable to remember what we'd argued about. That still happens when I argue with Anne.

Maybe I dissociate when trying to summon up the early Fred years. Or maybe I did at the time. Or maybe I can't recall what I really hadn't accepted as truth.

Or maybe I just have the memory of a stick of butter.

Chapter 40

Let's give me the benefit of the doubt and claim that I functioned over the next few years.

Lacking health insurance, I didn't visit the Boston experts frequently, but I made an effort to see them. I moved to a less expensive apartment. After Macy's, I worked at a public library, also part-time so I could write. And I commuted to the occasional consumer-testing job, evaluating people's feelings about everything from tomato sauce to presidential candidates.

I acquired a monthly gig with the Portsmouth newspaper writing about local travel, and, in a sign of enthusiasm for my new gay life, served as the unpaid New Hampshire editor for a regional LGBT newspaper. I signed on to create crossword puzzles for a state magazine that sadly never saw the light of day, and I taught humor-writing for UNH's continuing education program, the most memorable moment of which was when one member of the class asked me to provide her with a sense of humor.

I was busy. And I was poor.

So poor that I even tried for food stamps. But because I owned a car, which Alex had left me as he didn't want one in New York, I was rejected. I continued to get by, so broke I had to look up to see the poverty line.

And that exciting new lesbian life? Well, after what felt like forever, I started dating a woman who wound up displaying the emotional maturity of a dust bunny. But at least I learned that lesbian sex didn't scare me—no indeedy—and I went on to date other women.

I didn't think of myself as much of a prize, what with my new OCD diagnosis, my destitution and the piles of paper lining my living room. The latter I explained to visitors as the price of being interested in so many subjects, thereby putting a positive spin on a distinct negative. Or making a silk purse out of Fred's ear.

Not long after I was diagnosed I told my parents, and ultimately presented my mother with a book about OCD. I remember she read it quickly and didn't know what to make of it all. I allowed the subject to move to the back burner. Hell, I'm sure I even encouraged that, out of shame and ignorance. Over the next decades, I didn't bring my OCD up much, and my parents mentioned it even less.

They did help me pay for the Mass General appointments, and provided more financial assistance down the road. We all chose to think of that as necessary owing to a freelance writer's impecunious lot, and OCD was just a secondary reason.

Fred still hasn't forgiven me for that.

What I recall best is my father once wondering aloud if my OCD and sexual orientation were connected. He was none too subtly linking everything that was "wrong" with me.

For the record, my father, and my mother, eventually accepted my homosexuality. It was Fred we kept in the closet.

Chapter 41

At one point I interviewed to work part-time at a large local bookstore, a natural fit for a writer, right?

Unless the writer can't read.

The manager, noting on my resume that I'd gone to Colby, mentioned Richard Russo was teaching there. I didn't know that. I didn't know who Richard Russo was. His 1993 hit novel "Nobody's Fool" had eluded me. Consequently, so did the bookstore job.

It was becoming clear that I was missing out on things. Formerly an information junkie, I no longer had the reading ability to keep up with trends or stuff my head with historical trivia. Nor did I have the time—that junk mail wasn't going to quintuple-check itself.

I couldn't afford to buy music, or go to concerts, plays or movies very often. I couldn't buy books. (Yes, I wouldn't have been able to read more than a few anyway, but aspirational buying might've been nice.) With reading such a challenge, I didn't even check out many books from the library.

Except those children's books. I should've dazzled the bookstore manager with my knowledge of what was popular with the two to five set.

I'd come to understand that in essence I had three jobs: freelance writer, the part-time job of the moment and lackey of Fred. His daily demands that I check and hoard drained my time and energy as consistently as any other form of employment. And the skinflint never paid me.

I accepted that I'd have to work harder than others in this life. I still believed all the effort would lead to the writing future I wanted. That I might collapse from exhaustion on the way hadn't yet occurred to me.

My friends from school were well into careers and marriages and kids. My turning out to be gay put me on a different path. But it was Fred who put me on a dramatically different path.

I existed in survival mode. Make enough money to get by, try to continue writing, cope with the omnipresent anxiety by checking and keeping.

You might wonder why I didn't face the truth and pivot to some other profession so I could at least put the kibosh on the stress of living short on money and devoid of health insurance. An excellent question, if you do say so yourself.

I have several answers. Giving up a writing career would've felt like a failure; I believed if I just worked harder my finances would improve; change is difficult, even if it's good for you.

I thought I was facing the truth in acknowledging that I had an extra burden and would just need to put in more working hours than other people. I hadn't grasped the reality of how much time and effort Fred took from me. I was too busy, in the moment, trying to rid myself of the anxiety he created to step back and see how serious the problem was.

Like some appalling science-fiction creature, Fred was wound around my spine, so much a part of me that all that checking seemed necessary and normal. When a person, any person, is anxious, he or she tries to make the anxiety go away. Since I felt anxiety more frequently, and often with more intensity, than the average person, I had my hands full trying to assuage it.

In hindsight, I probably should've gone inpatient, racked up breathtaking medical debt trying to learn the skills to put Fred in his place.

As it was, I did my best. I appeared, for the most part, functioning to the outside world, and in important ways that was true. But because I appeased Fred more than I fought him, I was stressed, tired and as upwardly mobile as a duck with vertigo.

I assume it was this period, as I headed for my mid-30s, when I developed my go-to fantasy. Others fantasize about love, wealth, sex, a beach vacation. I fantasized that time would stop for everybody in the world—except me. Then I could catch up. I could write, and I could sort through accumulations, no matter how long it took. I was perfectly willing to work while everyone else on the planet was in stasis.

After all, I could take lots of naps. Who would know?

Chapter 42

Finally, even I felt the need to make a change. I longed to work full-time on a quiz book of Americana. My sister had lived in Washington state since college, and Kim had a large, quirky house on Whidbey Island. Even with one husband, four kids and assorted animals, she said there was room for me, too.

I was also motivated by wanting to see my nieces and nephews grow up. And by the sense that I'd exhausted New Hampshire's lesbian dating pool.

As I solidified my plans to move to the other coast, life proved it has the same ironic sense of humor as Fred. I met someone.

I told myself over and over that we couldn't get involved. I'd given notice at the library and to my landlord; I was bound for Washington. But I inconveniently fell for Heather anyway. In the summer of 1998 I drove across the country, my mother as my driving companion, firm in the belief that Heather and I could survive the distance if we wanted to. What a ninny.

At my sister's, I worked on the book. Slowly, of course. A factual mistake in any book would be bad, but in one testing nothing but knowledge of facts it would be fatal. So Fred and I plodded forward, while one of us pined for Heather.

Having a balky back, I visited Kim's chiropractor. The topic of my OCD must've come up, which is surprising, since I was more likely to admit to hemorrhoids than that. The doctor said she'd started providing something called brain adjustments, and they might benefit me.

I was skeptical. I'd seen an acupuncturist before who overflowed with confidence she could help me, but didn't budge Fred an inch. Still, I wasn't about to decline anything potentially useful, so I got a few treatments, which involved her putting her thumb on various nerve bundles to change the brain's electrical activity. Or something like that. I suspected I'd fallen into a pit of West-coast woo-woo.

But it worked. Or at least I felt better, more centered, for the rest of the day. I was in a place where I could sometimes fight Fred off, not need to check. The next day I'd be back to my normal, abnormal self. These brain adjustments, I thought, held some promise.

Longing overtook me, however, and Heather and I decided I'd return east. She flew to Seattle in the fall, and we drove back across the country, full of plans for our future together. A few months later she drop-kicked me. Shortest future ever.

Soon thereafter my mother developed a heart condition about which she grew anxious, so I didn't feel I could leave her alone to return to Washington. I lived in the family home for over a year and accompanied Mom to medical appointments, while also temping, writing and moaning to a therapist about my failed relationship.

I should've taken the opportunity to go through the mounds of paper and clothes and mementos I still had in my childhood bedroom. I did try, organizing a little here, purging a little there. Basically, though, I began the year 2000 chained to the same load of mostly unnecessary stuff. Fred, the show-off, proved he could dominate me in either millennium.

Chapter 43

After driving across the continent with my mother again—we were now experts at that—I fetched up at Kim's in the summer of 2000. While in New Hampshire, I'd longed to resume the brain adjustments, so that was my first order of business.

Whether it was happenstance or a deliberate decision on my part, I also finished off the last of my Prozac about this time. Chances are I wanted to see what my baseline was, and try the adjustments alone, unaided by pharmaceuticals. Sounds like the kind of gauntlet I'd throw down.

I received several treatments from the chiropractor, and before long I felt a real shift—in the wrong direction.

I saw with devastating clarity how bad my OCD was, and how much of my life I'd lost to it. I'd longed for the brain adjustments to rid me of Fred. Instead they wound up shining a spotlight on him.

I grew despondent over Fred's impact: I was poor, reliant on family and nowhere in my writing career. I felt the sting of being single while my ovaries threatened to wither. I still couldn't stop checking.

Perhaps if I'd stayed on anti-depressants I'd have managed a different perspective, something like this is a chance for a fresh start, and it's remarkable I've freelanced to the extent I have and my ovaries, while not youthful, are still under warranty.

But I bottomed out. I felt separate from the human race.

I became more suicidal than I'd ever been. I sat on my bed and asked myself how I could possibly go on.

But after a couple of days in this tortured place, I realized I couldn't scar my two nieces and two nephews like that. I journeyed across the country and moved in with them just to off myself? My last act on earth shouldn't be one that radiated pain.

I don't know whether my history of deciding against suicide to spare family members is proof of cowardice or my ingrained habit of putting their emotional welfare over mine. Either way, I'm still here. Which means Fred is, too.

Ultimately I confessed to my mother over the phone how bad things had gotten, and she called our old New Hampshire neighbor, who conveniently had served as the chairman of the psychiatry department at the University of Washington's medical school. He arranged for me to see his successor, and one of the two of them prescribed Prozac for me.

With no health insurance and no money, I had to charge it. This staying alive thing was infernally expensive.

Chapter 44

So there I was at my first appointment with the psychiatrist at the UW hospital. Discussing my suicidality with a perfect stranger. Because of that, and all that had led me to that moment, I left her office heavily dazed. As I drifted in a trance through the bustling lobby, a voice near me said, "I know you!"

Good thing somebody did, since I sure didn't.

It was an old friend from high school with whom I'd lost touch. I was thrilled to see her, after the fog had lifted enough for me to realize who the hell it was. We had a wonderful chat, during which she invited me to her wedding. I drove back to Whidbey Island, aware the vagaries of life had in that moment reduced my brain to Jiffy Pop.

The psychiatrist connected me with the UW's Outpatient Psychiatry Clinic, which was staffed by residents. I can't say for sure, but I have to assume my connection to the former department chair was the reason

I landed one of the coveted slots for free treatment. If after he'd pulled strings to get me into the system and I couldn't afford treatment and killed myself—well, that wouldn't have been a good look for anybody.

I began work with the head resident. Mick had been a surgeon, and had chosen to return to school to pursue a different path in medicine. He was smart, kind and had a sense of humor. I knew I was fortunate. I don't know how he felt.

Certainly he had one reason never to forget me. During a session on the morning of Feb. 28, 2001, we heard a substantial rumbling outside. "That's a big truck," Mick commented. The noise grew and the building began to shake, and we knew it was no truck. We both eyeballed the desk, realizing the two of us wouldn't fit under it. I looked at the ceiling, wondering if it was about to crash down on us. The rolling motions in the room slowed, a voice in the hall yelled for everyone to get out and Mick and I obliged.

It was the Nisqually earthquake. As a complementary therapy, I can't recommend it.

Chapter 45

It was Mick who suggested giving my OCD a name. If therapists usually direct children to do that, well, it was appropriate for me inasmuch as my recent journey to emotional Hades meant I was back to the beginning in fighting Fred.

You'll be shocked to learn that I still have much of the paperwork I generated from that time. Which happens to be terribly helpful in describing the work Mick and I did, so score one for hoarding disorder.

That paperwork reveals that Mick started me with a worksheet titled "Monitoring Your Automatic Thoughts." At the top of each I wrote "Checking" or "Hoarding," then briefly described the situation and on a scale of 0 to 100 assigned a level of initial anxiety.

I was in the early years of writing a humor column for LGBT newspapers around the country, so on one of these "Checking" sheets I scribbled my distress level was 75 as I wrote notes following a phone conversation with an editor. Then I listed my "Automatic Thoughts," which centered around my fear of inaccurately summarizing what he had said. I noted I tried to reconstruct parts of the conversation in my head. Repeatedly. At the bottom of the sheet was a list of emotions I could be feeling as I thought those thoughts. I checked off "anxious," "frustrated" and "irritated."

I wanted the old-fashioned "liverish" to be an option.

On a "Hoarding" sheet I tracked my attempt to throw out a months-old newspaper. Should've been a snap, since I rated it just a 40 to start. My listed thoughts indicated I'd saved the paper to spur column ideas. I had to look at every page to make sure it was safe to pitch. I spotted a story I could use. I kept that page. After checking that this was indeed the paper I just went through, I put it in recycling.

Yeah, a snap all right.

Rating anxiety between 0 and 100 is a favorite in OCD treatment. It's called the SUDS assessment, because you're measuring how great a lather you're in.

No, SUDS stands for Subjective Units of Discomfort Scale, and it figured prominently in the next homework assignments Mick gave me. I was allowed two glances at a piece of junk mail, then I assessed my anxiety, recorded it, tossed out the item, and every five minutes recorded my anxiety until it had reduced by half from the first assessment.

I averaged about a half hour of fretting over each credit-card solicitation and catalog before I felt I could get on with life.

When it came to my newspapers, I had to choose one at random, and divide it into three stacks according to importance. All the 3's, the least valuable, I wasn't allowed to read, and had to deposit immediately in the recycling, again marking my SUDS score every five minutes until I'd halved it.

Mick called this following the anxiety path, and it would've been appropriate and even festive had a nervous white rabbit in a waistcoat tripped down the path with me.

All too soon Mick had me tossing the stack of 2's as well. The 1's I brought into our appointments, where presumably Mick instructed me to whittle the pile down even further. If I can't remember just how that went, I'm confident a good time was had by none.

Although I'm equally sure I would've done my best to please, so there would've been a battle between Fred's desire to keep a three-month old news story and my desire not to fail in front of Mick. Which in itself was probably part of my OCD. Such a witches' brew.

These exercises Mick assigned me were to prove on a conscious level that the anxiety did go down over time, that I wouldn't spend the rest of my life fretting over a pitched Discover card offer, even if Fred told me I would. Which he did. Ad nauseum.

But this work was primarily meant to go deeper. We who check over and over have essentially worn grooves in our minds. This work is aimed at physiologically retraining the brain. Over time, initial SUDS rates go down the more you get used to, say, throwing out newspapers. It also takes less time for your anxiety level to drop.

That's the idea, anyhow. Being me, things haven't always worked out that way.

I must've made some progress, because on a sheet of paper I'd noted Mick's homework instructions were to toss all junk mail, apparently without checking, and to sort two newspapers, throwing out the 2's and the 3's. So it was conceivable by then that I could follow these instructions without tearing my hair out. Or his.

At the same time Mick told me to keep a daily OCD diary.

Oh, he had to know this wouldn't be pretty.

I wrote how I'd started at Sears at 9:00 in the morning, working on shoe markdowns, and checked some of them. How I filled in my timesheet and severely doubted the accuracy. How I bought something there and needed to check that both the sales slip and the change in my wallet were correct. Half an hour later I checked both again. When I got home in the afternoon I doubted an email

I sent was complete. Then I doubted the quality of my diary entry. I drove to the library, and upon my return checked that my library card was in my wallet, and that the items I brought back were now where they should be. I also had to review mentally what I'd dropped off there. Then I worried that I didn't explain the library entry completely correctly. I read a gay newspaper, and couldn't stick to Mick's rule of read three articles only. I put a section into recycling, then had to withdraw it to check, then put it back. I spotted a pen on the floor, and couldn't remember how it got there, so I worried I'd messed everything up. A few minutes later I fretted over why my keys were in my pocket. An hour later, when reaching for a knife in the drainboard, I feared I'd bumped and thereby wounded something else near it. By 10:00 that night I got off email and wrote in the diary that I was "afraid I've forgotten to put something where it goes, or somehow not finished finishing."

Living with Fred is hard enough. Tracking his activity rendered me incoherent.

If nothing else, the day's entry makes clear why OCD is known as the Doubting Disease.

I can't say whether Mick made me do the diary as a one-time exercise to highlight how much time I lost to Fred each day, or he meant me to continue doing it but realized the cure was worse than the sickness.

His hand-scrawled homework instructions make clear what came next: performing life tasks without checking. When I did laundry, I had to put the lid down and walk away and give myself a SUDS score. After buying groceries, I was to go home and shelve the groceries and rip up the receipt and give myself a SUDS score.

For encouragement, I had him write at the bottom something he said during the session: "There never was a completed task in the history of mankind," meaning any task could always be done better.

I also had him write another bit of motivation he'd stated: "There never was a human that performed perfectly." Except he left out the word "never." A mistake? A deliberate omission to prove his point? A joke? Don't mess with me like that!

Anyway, I set out to join the imperfect masses. I walked away from the washing machine, fighting with myself not to review the steps in my head. At the post office I threw away the receipt for stamps on the spot without checking it over. I returned from the library and didn't check my library card was in my wallet.

Such recklessness! Such abandon!

It took 20 to 40 minutes to halve my SUDS score. Sometimes I couldn't manage the assignment. I checked the laundry steps mentally, unable to stop myself. When I slid a check for the phone bill into an envelope, Fred heaped doubt on me, and I pulled the check out and analyzed and re-analyzed whether I'd written it correctly. Two days later, when trying to put a car payment in an envelope, I doubted the upside down piece of paper was really the check. I scanned the top part, realized I'd blown the exercise, so I checked every part of it, and noted that I "may as well complete the screw-up."

I suspect none of Mick's other clients provided so much exposition.

I took my act on the road when I returned to New Hampshire for Christmas of 2001. I emailed Mick a list of the vast contents of my old room. He told me go through as much as I could and divide into 1's, 2's and 3's. "Then in one fell swoop I want you to toss all of the pile of 3's. Do the 5-minute ratings only on tossing the entire HUGE pile of 3's. The stack of 2's also needs to go. You can do that the same day or wait one day but no longer."

I hope Santa brought me Xanax.

A couple of months later I had an experience I couldn't forget if I tried. Mick came to my apartment, along with a psychologist I knew somewhat, to help me purge paper. I sat there with them as we went through my files. They tried to convince me that old utility bills and car-repair records and paystubs could go. I agreed on some, haggled on others, refused on still others, my anxiety thermostat rising the longer this went on.

After what was probably 45 minutes but seemed like six hours, the guys left for their office, the black garbage bag they brought with them maybe half full. I returned to my chair, drained but entirely in the grip of an astronomical SUDS score. It occurred to me in that moment that I could call 911 and report I'd been robbed. Hey, the proof was in their back seat. Lots of paper with my personal information. I imagined flashing police lights, the psychiatrist and psychologist being pulled over, their struggle to explain.

It was an evil, but edifying, thought. Giggling helped relieve the anxiety. A bit.

I also remember another out-of-the-ordinary event. One day, instead of a normal session, I picked up Mick, and we proceeded to set out on my usual errands. At the library, after checking something out, I slid my library card in my wallet as Mick watched, and I didn't pull it back out again to check. We drove to the post office, and after the transaction I couldn't check my change or the receipt. The same at the grocery store.

In about a half hour we'd done three of my common errands; uncommonly, I hadn't checked anything. Not even once.

Which must've been why, after I dropped him back at his office, I sat in my car feeling there was an excellent chance I was going to faint. I never had before, but doing so much and checking so little had my head swimming. My head and my body felt like they'd parted company. The physiological reaction to not performing my normal checking rituals was downright dramatic.

I didn't faint, which was a shame, because I could've used the possibility of doing so as an excuse to check for the rest of my born days.

I see going through the old paperwork that Mick even had me make mistakes on purpose. I went nuts in the shoe stockroom at Sears, stacking boxes of shoes without regard to size one day, not slapping a sale price on a box another day. It was as close as I'll ever get to anarchy.

Eventually Mick left the University of Washington. I didn't drive him away; he actually finished his residency. His young replacement,

Ray, bravely gave me handouts on mindfulness and had me doing relaxation exercises. We listed my professional and personal goals and I noted which ones I worked on each day.

This practical approach was appropriate, as my finances were such that I'd begun going to the food bank.

We discussed ways of reducing my anxiety while I interviewed story subjects, including relaxation exercises before interviews, developing a shorthand and reminding myself that I don't have to be perfect. That suggestion I starred.

After about a year, Ray too went on to grander things. My notes from our final session feature phrases like "cognitive distortions," "obsession with perfection" and "overall low self-esteem." I assume those were matters he wanted me to continue working on. Either that or we spent our last meeting brainstorming band names.

The next resident, Kathleen, tried to get me to spend no more than ten seconds on each old newspaper page, which I did improve at over time. For another trip east to my loaded closets, she gave me a list of things to remember while trying to purge: "You've lived without it this long, so can probably live without it forever," and "You've done it before and survived, and you can do it again" and the pithy "When in doubt, throw out."

My notes from a session in July of 2004 are similar: "Don't have to purge everything—no ridiculous standards," and "Realize how much more going out than would've a few years ago" and "Have thrown out things like bills before and I'm not dead yet." It appears Kathleen and I were winding down, and the tone suggests to me that I was improving.

And then I got fired. The person in charge of deciding these things felt I'd occupied one of the free slots at the clinic long enough. Part of me understood. I'd been going for years, and I knew full well how many people out there needed help. But since I felt I was getting somewhere, the other part of me wanted to claw his eyes out.

Chapter 46

While writing the last chapter, I sent for my records from the University of Washington in order to establish the dates of when I saw whom. I also wanted to read how they described the treatment, and how they described me, knowing the latter could cause me distress.

It did. Perhaps it's for the best that I received only the records for my last year.

Those records began with an appointment in September of 2003 . . . with a fellow I don't even remember. Incredible.

It seems, after Ray moved on, that I took a summer break, and began again in September with a man named Paul, an MD and a PhD. Paul noted that I'd returned to the clinic for my free weekly psychotherapy session, that my previous week had been rough and I described struggling to get my work done and a lot of checking around financial matters.

He said that "Leslie still seems to be under control to her OCD and having more difficulties simply tolerating the stress she has when she does not check."

At least I was still trying not to check. No small thing, given the stress it caused.

Under the heading of "Physical Examination," Paul reported, "Her mood is dysphoric towards depressed . . . Her thought processes are logical and linear, although she has very poor insight into how her emotional reactions and how everyday events contribute to her OCD-like symptoms . . . Her insight into her disease is only fair and her judgment is again only fair."

Fair, fair, fair. I'd have flipped if I'd gotten that on a childhood report card.

Finally, under "Assessment," Paul opined, "It is difficult to ascertain what will now help Leslie, given the level of distress she has living without her OCD. She has numerous cognitive distortions and seems to cling to the idea that life will magically become 'all better' if her OCD and financial matters are straightened out."

Can I hate him now? Is that okay?

My life would've been much better, then and now, if Fred and finances weren't so problematic. That's not magical, that's fact, thank you very much.

But he was right about cognitive distortions. Roughly ten years after being diagnosed with Fred, and following a few years of hard work with therapists, I still believed that if I just stuck with my writing, just worked harder than others, I would succeed.

I remember one newspaper editor I was trying to convince to run my column telling me that he'd never known anyone so persistent. I spent years badly balancing writing with survival work, waiting for I-don't-know-what to happen, but believing it would.

On the one hand, with Fred impacting every aspect, it was an accomplishment to self-syndicate that biweekly column for a decade, and to work other parttime jobs that kept me afloat. On the other hand, it was a farce to remain dirt poor and without insurance on the strength of a faulty conviction that things would change.

I had one foot firmly in reality, and the other foot—well, distracted as I was by Fred's constant demands and the stress of living on the financial edge, that other foot was in Oz.

Paul's clinical notes from three weeks later state, "We discussed the role of free therapy and Leslie's discomfort with our therapeutic alliance. We have differing opinions on whether she is an appropriate free patient." So we were already at loggerheads about whether I should be receiving free treatment. I also felt he wasn't overburdened with sympathy. We agreed he'd try to transfer me to another resident.

A month later I saw him again for a short med-management appointment, which he was still providing for free. No other resident had thus far signed up for the joy of helping me. Paul mentioned in his notes that I'd lost one of my freelance writing gigs. "She is most reluctant to either get a job, apply for disability or get more financial support from her family."

This must've been a period between jobs when I was trying to get by on writing and housesitting. As to his disability suggestion, I viewed that as being for seriously disabled people and I couldn't accept that I was one of them. Nor did applying for disability gibe with my picture of myself as being one success away from the thrill of solvency. And I felt badly enough taking money from my mother—the thought of asking for more was nauseating.

But it was something else that really grabbed my attention while reading through Paul's old notes. There at the top of the report concerning our meeting on Nov. 5, 2003, he listed my "DSM-4 diagnosis": Obsessive-compulsive disorder and depression. Correct, obviously.

Then as some sort of companion condition he'd written "Narcissistic traits."

They heard my shriek in Tacoma.

Me? A narcissist? How can that be? How can you be a narcissist if you regularly dislike yourself? Isn't self-adoration one of the ground rules?

When I saw Travis recently, I rushed to ask if I struck him as a narcissist. "That does not describe you in any way, shape or form, in my view," he responded.

Whew.

No wonder Paul and I didn't get on if that's what he saw. Maybe it was that business of not, at that time, having an extra job. Maybe he saw my refusal as the world owes me, when really I was willing to be poor to do the work that mattered to me. I was just hanging on until I had a breakthrough. This was crappy thinking, but it wasn't narcissistic crappy thinking.

I'm certain there was also a lot of Fred involved in getting a job, each and every step loaded with fears, to say nothing of what the job itself would mean Fred-wise. Paul, it appears, didn't see the whole picture, and was impatient with me from the start.

When you've got a psychological condition or conditions, and you wade into the world of treatment, you always run the risk that you and your provider aren't a match. It's generally assumed that this is your fault, since you're the one who's crazy. But psychiatrists, psychologists, therapists and social workers are human, too, and experience everything from normal daily stresses to their own mental illnesses.

I'm not saying if the shrink spills his coffee on his chinos in the morning, he'll diagnose you with borderline personality disorder that afternoon. I'm saying all people are fallible and subject to bad moods and biases that they may or may not be aware of. Paul may simply not have liked middle-aged lesbians who drove maroon Mazdas.

In December we had our final appointment. The notes don't mention narcissism, but they do mention my "history of abuse of medications." MY WHAT?! I'd tried a number of meds prescribed for Fred, but I'd never abused any of them. Not even close. Was he confusing me with someone else? Was he delusional? Was HE on drugs?

He referred to the fact that I'd "terminated" with him "given a perceived incompatibility in our dyad." These notes prove our "dyad" was doomed. For a start, he was obviously hallucinating during our sessions.

Mercifully, a week later I started with Kathleen, and we were a much better fit. Kathleen's notes reflect my continued efforts to purge, my constant financial stresses, how I managed to interest *The Seattle Times* in a monthly column and how I may as well have been in a coma after that, so unwilling was I to pursue parttime work while I waited for the major daily newspaper's answer, which would be no.

I was ashamed to be making just $400 a month, and to be taking $500 a month from my mother. I figured out that even if all the newspapers that owed me money paid it, I'd still need some family assistance. I told Kathleen I was angry at myself for "not being in touch with reality."

Kathleen's notes summed things up this way after that session in June of 2004: "This is a 40-year-old woman with obsessive-compulsive disorder and major depressive disorder, recurrent. She remains somewhat stuck in her financial and work situation, and has been realizing even more now that she may have been unrealistically hoping to survive on her small freelance writing income. We did not get to discuss this new insight in depth because, as a defense, she often brings up troubling information at the very end of the session."

Now there's a helpful trait.

The following week, reported Kathleen, I spoke of lacking self-sufficiency, and what a number that had done on my self-esteem. I was connecting the dots, even if the connections had long been as obvious as pink-eye to other people.

In July we spoke of my impending move to a new apartment and how I hoped not to move a lot of hoarded paper with me. Kathleen wrote, "We discussed how Leslie has come a long way since coming to this clinic about three years ago when she would not have been able to even consider doing this move and throwing out her papers."

A month later, we had our final session. As I mentioned in the previous chapter, someone in power had decided I could no longer fill up one of the free care slots with the psychiatry residents. As I also mentioned, I understood that. But as Kathleen's notes show, we both thought I was improving. Such a shame to quit at that point.

I just bet it was Paul.

Chapter 47

Reading Kathleen's notes reminded me that she and I also dealt with one of my break-ups. I'd been dumped by a therapist, Lucy, for another woman, so that upped my anxiety ante. What's noteworthy now about that relationship is its beginning. On just our second date I confessed to Lucy that I had OCD. Apparently I wanted to get that bit over with.

She responded, "Everybody has something." I was half in love right there.

Anybody who's ever dated, let alone anybody with a mental illness, knows about the confession stage. When do you come clean with that part of you that you don't like or that the other person might not like? In this case, I dispensed with it early. Sometimes people do it on, say, the fifth date, or after getting engaged or . . . in the afterlife.

Loathing Fred as I did, Lucy's nonchalant response was both a surprise and freeing. Now I could just be myself with her. Of course, that turned out to be insufficient. Later I heard through the grapevine that Lucy, struggling financially herself, had panicked about my insolvency and turned to someone who could literally be more supportive. So in that sense Fred did have a hand in our demise. But of course he did, the wee meddling bastard.

I recall another time I bared my soul. It was shortly after I moved to Seattle in 2000, and I'd connected with another lesbian recent transplant to the area. She and I became friends, and I decided to tell her I had OCD. She responded, "Not another one!"

That day I learned we're everywhere, ruining the general ambience wherever we go.

Chapter 48

I can't remember exactly when I did this. After falling to pieces upon my return to Washington? During the therapy with the UW residents? But I wrote an email to family and friends telling them about my struggles with Fred and how low he'd brought me.

Some recipients hadn't even known about Fred, and nobody knew what a bad case I had. I'd reached a point where hiding my illness was too much of a burden; and I realized I needed emotional support. As one who had formerly projected control and preferred to be a support to others, going public was no small thing.

I'm sure I still have a physical copy of that email, along with responses I got back. But I don't know where they're buried. I could open every box and search, but that will take more time and create more of a mess than the rebuilding of the Notre-Dame cathedral.

So I can't verify this, but something makes me think I actually misspelled "hoard" as "horde" in the letter. Me, the checker, misspelled one of the most critical words. Had I known at the time, I'd have been aghast and berated myself for weeks. Now I try to appreciate the irony. I also enjoy the image I've created of Genghis Khan's hordes overrunning villages for the sole purpose of hoarding their newspapers.

Because writing that confessional was out of character, I wasn't sure what to expect. The responses were uniformly kind. But one woman, a good friend since high school and one of the most sensible people I've ever known, didn't write back. Thinking my email might've gone astray, I dropped her another line. No answer.

I got her message. She didn't want to have anything to do with me.

From the start, I had such strong feelings of shame about being mentally ill. My old friend's reaction suggested those feelings were entirely appropriate.

Coming out as gay over the last two decades hasn't been terribly hard for me, in large measure because I've felt that was nothing compared to what I really had to hide. With OCD and hoarding disorder, who has time to be ashamed over queerness?

It's worth mentioning that when I came out as a lesbian, I also lost one friend . . . who ricocheted back a few weeks later, admitting she'd feared that being seen with me would lead others to think she was gay.

I'm pretty sure the friend who dropped me over Fred didn't fear guilt by association. Maybe I was no longer the person she'd known, or my condition was too weird, or she felt I'd be an emotional burden or she just didn't know how to handle it.

Occasionally I've wished I could send Fred to visit her and explain. But that's obviously impossible. He knows if he left me alone he'd be losing out on frequent annoyer points, and after all these years together he's this close to a world cruise.

Chapter 49

When Kathleen at UW and I ended our sessions on August 16, 2004, she gave me a copy of the clinic's referral list. I tried to connect with some of the mental health centers and individual providers on the list without success, and I suspect after being rebuffed a few times I allowed myself to become consumed with just getting by.

I'll say it: Over the next few years I was shrink-less in Seattle.

I cobbled together something close to a living with writing, housesitting and a return to library work.

Fred remained the Krazy Glue. Though I made an effort to continue the better habits I'd learned in therapy, inevitably, without someone riding herd on me, they slipped away. I still needed someone to check that I wasn't—at least, not repeatedly.

I hadn't absorbed to my marrow that the only way around Fred was through. He wouldn't disappear with time, and no drug would rid me of him. Halfway measures in therapy wouldn't cut it, either. Heaven knows it never seemed like I was doing things halfway. I went to my appointments. I dutifully kept up with the homework, even though it felt like whacking a pinata full of wasps.

The hard work I managed wasn't enough, and it didn't stick. I returned to survival mode, visiting a clinic for the broke to receive Prozac and basic medical care. I hung on for a better day professionally, assuming, by the law of averages, that it would show itself if I endured.

Fred didn't give a fig for the law of averages. He knew he'd made my life a trial for years, and he fully intended to carry on. If I believed I inevitably had to succeed at some point after so much failure, he, the swine, believed failure suited me down to the ground.

Chapter 50

As has become clear by now, I received help along this lonely journey. I'm grateful to my parents, sister and a friend who provided financial assistance. In hindsight, yes, I realize it could be argued they enabled me, that had they withheld aid I might've been forced into a quicker reckoning.

Could be. Don't care. They were there when I needed them.

I'm thankful to the local food bank, and the affordable medical clinic. And then there was a non-profit organization that paid for dental work I badly needed. I won't forget that charitable group because I'm appreciative and also because of the humiliation involved.

Around the time I was winding down with Kathleen at UW, I contacted Washington Women in Need. I told the staffer that I made about $800 a month, and received $500 from my family. That last bit, she informed me, put me over their income limit.

I hung up, dazed. I spent the next 15 minutes gauging how desperate I was for crowns on two teeth. Pretty damn desperate, I decided, and called back. I told her the truth, that it had been pride talking, and I wasn't making more than $500 a month. "I've heard two different stories within an hour," she said. Mortified for having fibbed, and for the actual size of my writing income, I told her I understood her quandary, and waited for her to dismiss me. Instead she retrieved my file; ultimately I received the grant. And the crowns.

Organizations that serve the needy have no guarantee their clients will ever progress to self-sufficiency. Certainly that's often the hope, but frequently not the outcome. I say to them now, thank you; it looks like I'll make it; I'm sorry it took longer than I expected; I tried to be a decent person along the way.

Fred's still with me, you understand. But these days I have a more realistic sense of his impact and how to fight him. You helped prop me up till I got here.

Lest you entertain any doubt, Fred has no interest in being a decent anything.

I'll round off this chapter on gratitude by adding I'm thankful for Prozac. Though it accomplishes diddly-squat where Fred is concerned, it's long helped me with depression, and that counts for a lot.

My goal now is to live long enough to see scientists make Prozac taste like Belgian chocolate.

Chapter 51

In the summer of 2007, something went right: I met Anne. She wasn't scared off by Fred, which of course earned her a huge checkmark in her favor. A widow, she actively wooed me, which didn't hurt either, and her big heart for the world and the less fortunate in it drew me in. Before long, I was staying at her place most nights, though we didn't officially cohabitate for two years, in clear defiance of lesbian stereotype.

Shortly after I moved into Anne's mid-century modern home, with its two dogs and two cats—that part was in clear alignment with lesbian stereotype—we registered as domestic partners with the state of Washington, in large measure so I could go on Anne's insurance.

Well, blow me down, or better yet Fred. I was covered at last.

Unfortunately, the reportedly best place in town for OCD didn't take insurance. Even if you get up the gumption to battle OCD and/

or hoarding, and even if you're insured, it's too often the case that treatment is still prohibitively expensive.

I'd like to say all the Freds out there got together on another plane of existence—or maybe in Atlantic City—and hatched a plot to ensure their survival by arranging for therapy to be financially out of reach. It's a fun, if paranoid, idea. In truth, with making money at the heart of the American health-care system, rather than making people better, that priority keeps a lot of people from access to mental health services. But that's too aggravating to dwell on, so I'll continue to hold a picture in my head of all the Freds drinking Mai Tais and brainstorming dastardly ideas on a whiteboard.

Though the Evidence Based Treatment Center of Seattle didn't accept insurance, it turned out my insurance would reimburse for a portion of each visit, so on March 25, 2010, I presented myself to begin working with a psychologist named Miles. I was in fact fortunate to get in, since the EBT Center, pricey as it was, always had a waiting list. Which shows how many Freds were running amok in the Puget Sound region.

Strangely, I've found limited notes from my sessions with Miles. Either Fred the hoarder lay down on the job, or that written material resides in a box I've been uninclined to open.

I do remember the crux of what we did, but let's first take a brief excursion through some more abbreviations. Cognitive Behavioral Therapy (CBT) is an umbrella term for methods therapists use to help people learn to identify and change destructive thought patterns that negatively impact behavior and emotions. Exposure and Response Prevention (ERP) is the CBT of choice where Fred is concerned.

So the gold standard CBT for OCD is ERP.

I apologize most humbly for subjecting you to that sentence.

With ERP, the sufferer is exposed to situations that make her anxious, but she doesn't perform a compulsion to make the anxiety go away. Instead she sits with the anxiety, on the therapist's promise that, eventually, the same situation won't be so nerve-wracking.

Who wouldn't sign up for the chance to subject herself to a stream of anxiety from morning to night, with no legitimate way of making the fear go away, all because that smug therapist claims that at some unknown point in the future she might not feel so crazy?

Talk about a tough sell.

If the particulars of ERP sound familiar to you, that's because it was ERP the UW residents inflicted on me. At that time, I was so nervous and mired in my old ways I didn't grasp the full picture of the disease or the way to fight it. By the time I got to Miles at the EBT Center, I was more amenable. Not as pliable as, say, Gumby, but more receptive on the whole.

Since Anne and I received a daily newspaper, Miles had me skim it instead of reading most of it, so I could be done with the paper before the season changed. We employed the SUDS scale, but rather than take my anxiety temperature every five minutes as I had with Mick, Miles wanted me to assign a number before I began, then my peak number while skimming, and finally a number after I finished.

Those post-skimming numbers went down, meaning I became more comfortable with the notion of possibly having missed information. The numbers didn't plummet, but they did descend. In genteel, lady-like fashion.

I confessed to Miles about another manifestation of Fred, fearing I'd injured a dish if I hit it against another. So when I removed the dishes from the dishwasher and put them in the cupboard, I was forbidden from being careful about bumping them. My peak numbers decreased, despite feeling like a literal bull in a not-literal china shop.

At another point, with the same put-upon dishwasher, Miles told me I could perform each step of starting a load of dishes only once, and as the capper I had to leave the bottle of dish soap out of place. All this was to expose myself to the fear that if I don't do every step, and perfectly, the dishes won't get clean.

Miles also said, when it came to the stove, that I needed to turn it off, check one time visually, then walk out of the kitchen. Since the fear that the stove is on and unattended is popular with OCD sufferers, I've often mused that somewhere out there a therapist has given this directive only to have a house burn down. Then what? The therapist gets OCD?

To combat my need to check in other areas, I brought into our sessions index cards, envelopes, an address book and stamps. I wrote a sentence or two on a card, placed it in an envelope, addressed, stamped and sealed the envelope, without checking any of the steps. Miles dropped the envelopes into the building's outgoing mail, and they winged their way around the country, to friends and family I trusted to be willing recipients.

I sent so much mail a friend who lives on a Maine island reported, "Our postmistress is starting to wonder."

I can't recall whether I experienced any benefit from this exercise, but I suspect Miles did, as he had plenty of time to plan his grocery list while I scribbled.

One of the most important things I got from Miles was the most obvious. I still hadn't twigged that the slow pace at which I read even for fun was a symptom of Fred. Maybe I needed an OCD expert to confirm it. I don't know, but it felt like a revelation. Miles spoke of ways to tackle the issue, like reading with an instrument that forces you to read one line at a time, or reading with a piece of cardboard in hand to cover what I'd read and prevent me from going back.

We didn't spend much time on this. Other Fred habits seemed more pressing. I think for me it was enough to know that yet another shortcoming was actually Fred.

Besides, with all those index cards to mail, I was busy continuing to prop up the U.S. Postal Service. I fully expected a certificate of appreciation from the postmaster general.

Chapter 52

While not in therapy, I'd been getting Prozac via my regular doctor. Now Miles connected me with a psychiatrist named John to parcel out the Prozac. John also suggested I try some other options.

I gave the antidepressant Celexa a go, but it put weight on me more effectively than a daily hot fudge sundae.

I moved on to another antidepressant, Wellbutrin, which initially gave me feelings of euphoria. They didn't last long, wouldn't you know. Soon I was teary, irritable and nauseated. I needed an antidepressant for my antidepressant.

After I reported this range of impacts to John, he agreed that I could reduce the dosage. The next day I woke up suicidal. God, my life was pathetic: A big day for me was one that saw a low SUDS score. What a joke. I was done with the struggle. Fred wins.

Because of my prior bouts with suicidality, I recognized what was happening, which helped moderate the despair. But I remained the soul of irritability, and Anne made me promise to call John.

Prozac and Celexa work by increasing the levels of serotonin in the brain. Wellbutrin works differently, and for me, not at all. Clearly I needed a pharmaceutical that would be a Trevi Fountain of serotonin.

As I noted earlier, Prozac helps me with depression, but it doesn't touch Fred, so I sampled these other meds in the hope that one would reduce my OCD. None did in any noticeable way, and boy oh boy, those side effects.

Anne had to endure the irritability the Wellbutrin wrought, but one side effect she enjoyed. I can't remember whether it was Celexa, Wellbutrin or something else I might've tried, but for a short period a drug sent my libido into overdrive.

In my experience, positive side effects soon vanish, while negative ones attempt to outlive you.

Chapter 53

Eventually Miles moved across the country for what he said was a great professional opportunity. The next brave psychologist to take me on was Sally.

If I have few written records for my work with Sally, I do have an exhortation she wrote still attached to my bulletin board: "Keep the 1s—Everything else is just taking up space!"

Words to purge by.

Sally and I unearthed a discovery. I realized one of the main reasons for my needing to keep unnecessary paper is a huge desire for completeness—I want to have available every bit of research I did for a story, and every draft of the story to be able to see how I changed it. I want a record of every medical appointment, in the form of notes or a paid bill. It's not the big picture I'm after, it's the entire, fleshed-out, details-included picture. There's safety in that for me.

The irony? Keeping all this paper makes it impossible to find a blessed thing.

The Fred grooves are worn into my brain, but this hoarding eye-opener gave me something to battle on a conscious level. No, I don't need to keep every Christmas card from this friend to see how her kids have grown over the years. What else would I expect them to do?

Like Miles, Sally, too, moved on. She wound up leaving not just the EBT Center, but the field of mental health.

I felt like the Typhoid Mary of psychology.

My psychiatrist, John, left his practice—but not his career, let it be noted. The EBT Center added a psychiatrist to its staff, so it was easy to sign on with Sara. And when Sara moved to Spokane, I began working with Karen, as I continue to do.

After decades of being in the world of psychologists and psychiatrists, I've made two observations. First, these experts keep getting younger. Second, I doubt these folks change jobs or careers more often than other professionals—it can just be wrenching for their clients when they do, given the intimacy of the working relationship and the anxiety already at play.

I started working with Travis at the EBT Center in 2015. If he leaves . . . I'm going with him.

Chapter 54

Miles alerted me to the existence of a peer-led group in Seattle for OCD sufferers that met one Saturday every month at a downtown hospital. Miles and his fellow psychologists at the EBT Center took turns doing presentations for the group. Family and friends were welcome to attend, so Anne and I decided to give it a try.

On our first visit, the leader began the meeting and promptly introduced himself as Fred. I realized I could laugh, bolt or throw up.

Over the years since, no matter how politely I ask, Fred has stubbornly refused to change his name.

Fred and his wife, Pam, are the longtime stalwarts of OCD Seattle, organizing and running the meetings, and maintaining the email list. Fred's manifestations of his Fred are numerous. As he likes to say when he opens meetings, "OCD was just dripping off my fingers." He got into therapy, saved his marriage and now helps others cope.

Fred has attendees introduce themselves, and when I first began going, I introduced myself as a person with OCD whose primary symptoms were checking and hoarding. When the DSM-5 came out in 2013, I then had to introduce myself as a person with two afflictions, OCD and hoarding disorder. If the next version of the DSM subdivides me into a third diagnosis, I'll have to quit going to the group.

Pam and Fred had to adapt as well, changing the name of the group to Seattle OCD and Hoarding Disorder Support Group. More accurate definitions in the mental health field meant a wordier appellation.

As many as 50 people attend the meetings, which generally follow a pattern. Everyone starts out together for the presentation, then we break up into smaller groups: people with OCD, hoarders or friends and family. I had to decide between two sub-groups, and I can assure you I wasn't the only one spoiled for choice.

In the friends and family gathering, folks, naturally, vent about us, share resources and offer or seek support. Anne tried to be helpful to, say, a father whose adult son needed to spend much of the day reciting prayers, or a grandmother who feared her grandchildren were acting out in response to their mother's OCD.

The relevant question is where family members are in their own journey. If parents have a teenage son who showers three times a day and has just been diagnosed with OCD, they may be wanting to learn about treatment options. If an adult daughter can't open her mother's front door for all the stuff piled behind it, she might need to cry. If a sister can't take her brother's asking for reassurance one more time, she might need . . . a vacation.

Having a family member with OCD isn't for the faint of heart. If you don't feel the same overpowering impulses, you don't understand what's happening. You want to yell, and probably have yelled, "Just stop it!" Medications aren't necessarily helpful. Therapy doesn't always work, and it's hard and expensive and time-consuming. Why not just ignore the illness? Heaven knows the sufferer often prefers that.

Because life with the OCD in control is even worse than the pain of fighting it. Dammit.

I found myself hoping that Anne would hear some of the stories in the friends and family support group and realize our lot could be worse. At least I was aware of my Fred. At least I was fighting him by taking drugs, going to therapy, doing my homework and attending this group.

I'm pretty sure Anne has never seen an upside to the situation.

Over time it became clear to me what individuals, both sufferers and their loved ones, get out of attending the Seattle OCD and Hoarding Disorder Support Group. Especially for those not in therapy, this is a chance to absorb insight from experts, and practical suggestions from those in the same boat. If you're a sufferer whose family refuses to engage, or a family member whose loved one refuses to seek help, you can obtain some sorely needed succor.

Above all, attending the group makes it crystal clear that you aren't alone.

Fred—the living, breathing one—likes to suggest in his opening remarks that staying after the meeting for the potluck lunch provides an opportunity to talk to a person who mentioned something that resonated with you. A conversation can start like this: "Gee, you said you worried about picking up a knife and stabbing someone. Me too! Have an eggroll."

I made a point of spending one lunch talking to a guy with whom I had nothing in common. He was a half-Black, half-Cherokee heterosexual Christian who grew up without indoor plumbing in rural North Carolina. He worked as a garbageman, and during the meeting he'd spoken of needing to check that he's emptied the bins so often that by lunchtime he's finished only a quarter of his route instead of half. He spoke of the anxiety being volcano-like.

We had everything in common.

I don't think he returned to the group. I hope I didn't scare him off, since I do seem to have that effect on psychologists. It's not unusual for people to come once and not show up again. This is tough stuff.

Life circumstances can keep you away, of course. I stopped going for a lengthy stretch when finances dictated that I pack glassware at Crate & Barrel on Saturdays.

Just think of all the reasons persons could come up with early on Saturday not to attend the meeting: you'd rather sleep some more, or you don't want to drive all the way downtown, or your need to unplug everything in the house always makes you late, or you failed to meet the goal you set the previous month in your small group, or last time you spotted a suspicious stickiness on one of the meeting-room tables, or you have sex-related symptoms you're too embarrassed to tell others, or you really, really don't have the energy to face your demons today.

It's a wonder anybody goes at all.

Chapter 55

Fred, the group leader, as opposed to Fred, the bane of my existence, likes to say, "OCD is limited only by the human imagination," an insight of OCD specialist Dr. Jonathan Grayson. The manifestations are so diverse, with sufferers obsessing over everything from germs to symmetry to sexual orientation to morality. Further, a person's obsessions can morph over time, which just about hollers that OCD is less about the issue of the moment, and more about the anxiety itself.

A key point. And one that's damned difficult to grasp when your internal voice is demanding you brush your teeth to a count of 39 or your parents will die.

One of the more remarkable things I've noticed in going to the local OCD group is, despite how compelling our obsessions are to us, sometimes we have little patience with the obsessions of others. Fred remembers the time a fellow laughed at some of his obsessions, and Fred took a piece of cheese, dropped it on the floor, picked it up and popped it into his mouth. He watched as all the color drained from the man's face, leaving him a less than fetching shade of gray.

If you have contamination issues, don't mess with Fred.

I've heard a full-blown hoarder describe as odd the hoarding-related idiosyncrasies of another. I wanted to say something about glass houses, but the image of any of us hoarders living in a see-through home was so frightening it stopped me cold.

I'm not immune to this impatience. I can be short with someone unwilling or unable to grasp the intensity of his condition. Presumably I'm mired in a delightful case of projection.

We sufferers have these sicknesses that make us do strange things. There's just gradation and variation to the strangeness. I suspect being unforgiving with each other sometimes stems from feeling so badly about ourselves that we need to feel superior to someone. Other times we're so mired in the stress of our own obsessions that we can't pull back and see the illness, and that my illness is your illness is their illness.

At any rate, intolerant OCD victims and hoarders make me think of racist LGBTQ folks, when those who've faced egregious discrimination choose to discriminate. I always hope the experience leads to the opposite result.

One thing I can say for my Fred and his cronies is that they don't have a discriminatory bone in their invisible bodies: They ruin everyone's lives equally. The group, like Seattle itself, is largely white, but sufferers and family members of every hue have regularly sought it out, and I'm not the only queer person who attends.

Mental illness as uniter. Swell.

Chapter 56

As I've become more likely to admit my OCD to others, I occasionally hear the same confession back. Some years ago I discovered that
my hairdresser, Kimm, is also afflicted. As I sat in her chair while she
snipped, she told me of an incident that was all too fresh in her mind.
She went to check that her front door was locked at night, as she'd done
a zillion times before, and found it unlocked. Shocked, Kimm blew up
at her husband. I told her I react similarly when I discover Anne has
thrown out something she shouldn't.

I declared, "It would all be so much better if they would just do what
we say," and we laughed so hard I'm lucky I still have two ears.

Kimm didn't know about the concept of naming your OCD, so I
explained how mine came to be called Fred. She instantly decided hers
would be Sam. "Sam and Fred," I said. "We sound like an R&B duo."

The teenage daughter of a friend of mine was recently diagnosed with OCD, and I've found myself wanting to grab the kid and hurl her bodily into an inpatient program. Naturally this is because I've had Fred so long and lost so much to him that I don't want her to suffer the same fate. I want to tell her to fight it now! Fight it now so it won't steal your life.

Instead I downplay any advice to my friend with "Take it for what it's worth," and ask after her daughter infrequently, casually. Impressive restraint, considering I want to kidnap the girl.

When it comes to people I encounter going about my daily life, I'm quick to spot the signs. Tasked with taking the office's certified mail to the post office, I've twice now listened to a man at the counter describe each step as he performs it: "I run this through the machine. I stamp it. I give it back to you." In processing my mail and reassuring himself that he's taken every required action, he's really performing two jobs. Alas, he's paid for only one.

I often visit a branch of Wells Fargo, where a certain teller deals with the KS deposit slowly, all the while making more than the usual amount of small talk. My guess is he's buying time to check mentally, invisibly, just as I used to do when working at a library front desk. Of course, the fellow might simply be excessively friendly. But I'd put my money, If I had any, on OCD, and the notion that it takes one to know one.

I've come close to asking this young Asian-American bank employee if he has OCD. But the possibility of giving offense is so great. "Hey, dude, do you have a mental illness?" There's the chance I'm right and the question leads him to salvation. There's also the chance I'm wrong—or right—and the question leads me to the emergency room.

Chapter 57

My friend Mary, not a sufferer, actually had a serendipitous OCD experience. A friend of hers with OCD came over to visit. The friend took one look at Mary's well-used kitchen and asked if she could clean it. Instead of being offended, Mary exclaimed, "Hell yes!" A win-win, in my opinion.

I'd never claim OCD is worth having, but occasionally it can be useful.

When I started working at KS in 2013, the plan was for me, like the others in the office, to go out and see elderly or disabled clients and pay their bills for them, gather their tax information, etc. But I began to realize that my co-workers were all so busy with their clients that office needs were being neglected. The billing was so scattershot we sometimes didn't have enough money in the bank to cover our paychecks. The boss had the heart of a saint but couldn't keep her appointments organized if her life depended on it. The place needed an office manager. This was a job for . . . Fred.

I instituted monthly billing and handle all the deposits, so now the business is flush. I keep track of the boss's calendar. I make sure our bills are paid on time and that we don't carry a credit card balance. KS needed Captain Anal, and there I was.

As it happened, Lady Loosey Goosey was there, too. Her name is Sandy, and as obsessed as I am with detail, Sandy has never met a detail she couldn't ignore. To pore over her bills is to tear out my hair, as I plod through missing dates, descriptions and time worked. Last month, after a joint expedition through one of her invoices, she said, "You're very good at catching everyone's errors. Thank you for doing that." I reviewed her tone for facetiousness, but heard none. If Captain Anal and Lady Loosey Goosey can exist in the same office, there's hope for the Middle East.

The trade-off for putting up with Sandy's laissez faire attitude toward detail is the fact that she's an absolute hoot, and terrific with our hardest cases. She can sweet-talk or cajole an 80-year-old with a fear of hospitals into getting a prostate exam.

KS's trade-off for my diligence at keeping the company afloat? I'm slow. A well-educated marmoset could put those deposits together faster.

The best example I've ever heard of OCD actually being helpful came from a therapist in private practice who spoke to the Seattle OCD group. So many therapists don't know how to treat OCD, but she did, motivated in part because her brother had it. And it was a good thing he did, because his job in the military was to oversee nuclear weapons.

By God, that's a case where OCD should be a job requirement.

Chapter 58

In most professional settings, OCD is emphatically not useful. It put the kibosh on my journalism career. It can do a number on anyone's career, whether, like me, you need to check everything you do multiple times, or you can't even get to work because you have so many rituals to perform at home.

I've given it thought, and perhaps the world's worst job for me—aside from math teacher—would be basketball referee. Picture me in the early minutes of a game, blowing my whistle. "You double dribbled. I think. Looked that way. Maybe not. I need to see it again. Can you recreate for me what you just did? No? Well, do you think you double dribbled? No? Let's ask your coach."

My capacity for doubt and need to get it right would lead to bedlam on the court.

On the other hand, maybe a ref is exactly what I should be. Talk about intensive therapy, making and sticking to quick decisions, one after another.

By halftime, I'd be the one wheeled out on a gurney.

And nobody would be sorry.

Chapter 59

Fred's been a robust pain in the ass these last five-and-a-half years as I've handled my mother's affairs. I wrote in Chapter 20 that she had a stroke at age 80, and she's now 86.

I'm 26⁷. Being her Power of Attorney has aged me.

After the stroke occurred, my family hoped mightily that Mom would regain some of what she'd lost. That didn't happen. The stroke was so severe her entire right side went on strike, and she became wheel-chair-bound. Worse, she lost a hefty portion of her cognitive ability. Mom has been largely unable to converse, to track, to remember.

Not surprisingly, she never accepted that. Each day she wades through the newspaper, spending the whole morning on it, which beats even me. But she retains next to nothing, and has no idea she keeps re-reading the same stories. Reading the newspaper isn't just habit, it's part of her illusion that she's still functioning.

She insisted on remaining at home, so we made it happen, hiring caregivers. For years I paid those bills, and her other bills, but in order to give her as much agency as possible, we allowed bank statements and similar papers to go to her, so she could look at them and have some semblance of involvement in her own affairs. That made my life more difficult, not getting all the information, but my siblings and I bought into propping up her sense of self. Delusion as a group effort.

You might be wondering how I did with much of her mail coming to me, on top of my own. The answer is: mixed. Her mail did too often join my piles. One of my biggest failures was not opening an envelope from her long-term insurance company that contained two reimbursement checks. Something, maybe taxes or an accounting from the company, made me realize what had probably happened, and I forced myself to hunt down and open all relevant unopened mail. Fred had never had so much fun, as I experienced double the usual mail-opening anxiety plus a hefty dose of self-loathing.

He still remembers that day fondly.

I found the expired checks and called the company, which agreed to reissue them. I heard in my head a medley of past therapists telling me most mistakes could be fixed, and the therapist mélange got it right. Making a mistake doesn't always lead to ruination.

That part Fred would prefer to forget.

Because in my adult life Fred has kept me poor and fixated on things that don't matter, I've never bought a house or had a child or taken a number of steps expected of an American adult with my background. I went without health insurance for so long I knew little about how it actually worked. Between bureaucratic inexperience and a Fred-based terror of screwing up paperwork, I'm a lousy choice to be in charge of someone's affairs.

But, for the most part, I've managed. Take that, Fred.

Over these last years, I found myself in a host of unexpected situations. I battled with a caregiving company that lied to us about being licensed, which caused the insurance company to deny repayment. I fixed the messes Mom made when she induced caregivers to drive her to the bank. I've secured her tax materials each year from hither and yon. I've dealt with liquidating Mom's assets, one painfully after another, in order to pay for her care.

In addition to all the layers of Fred involved, allow me to point out that a lot of this stuff involved math. Because of course it did.

Fortunately for me, I wasn't alone. Anne offered solace. My colleagues, with many combined years working with elders, provided advice, and my boss, recognizing my head was going to explode, which would add nothing to the office decor, figured out some particularly sticky accounting for me.

My brother Patrick and sister-in-law Julie, who live near Mom, did yeoman's work fixing whatever broke in the house, tending to the car and visiting as often as possible. My sister Kim, who like me still lives in Washington state, scoured the internet for medical supplies and comfortable clothes, flew across the country regularly and, when it became clear on one of her visits, about four years after the stroke, that Mom was no longer safe in her house, hustled to find her a suitable home.

For which I, of course, had to fill out all the paperwork. I discovered I'd rather mediate a dispute between caregivers any day of the week.

We were greatly relieved when Mom moved into assisted living. The staff at Valley Terrace would make sure she ate and drank and took her meds, and would have eyes on her all the time.

Mom, on the other hand, was furious. We were forcing her to leave her home. Damn straight we were. Any other course would've been irresponsible. She even told at least one visitor to her new abode that we were trying to kill her.

I knew that was the stroke talking, but it was still hard to hear, since we were, in fact, trying to do the opposite. It was an ironic bookend to my young years spent trying to protect her.

On each visit east, I shredded old papers and donated books and generally tried to purge Mom's house of stuff no longer relevant. Yes, I did this slowly, carefully, always sorry I couldn't get to more. Fred was upset I got to any at all.

I was startled to find a copy of "Buried in Treasures," a self-help book well-known to hoarders. Did Mom think she was a hoarder? Did someone else think so? Did she get it for me and forget to mail it? A person combing through a parent's possessions sometimes finds shocking or mysterious items. Instead of a letter from an old boyfriend, I found a 182-page paperback I can't explain. Not nearly as fun as a steamy diary, but certainly a mystery to me.

The sorting process underscored what I already knew, namely that in her later years Mom became obsessed—and I don't use the word lightly—with natural solutions to health, particularly in the form of supplements. Kim had already cleared out the bottles and bottles of pills; I purged the mail and newsletters and books in which Mom had invested so much time and money. Before her stroke, she would complain to Kim and me about how busy she was with "paperwork." It took us a while to recognize that "paperwork" mostly meant mail from these alternative health outfits, some of them dubious. Mom felt obliged to read through all that material, rather than attend to tasks she'd said she wanted to after retiring, like sorting the family photographs.

Just as I once felt compelled to spend so much time cutting out magazine stories, or as I still feel compelled to keep old medical bills or to check KS's checking account online daily or to reread passages in books or to doubt endlessly whether what I wrote is accurate, my mother and I share overarching anxiety that misplaces our priorities and prevents us from enjoying life.

Maybe I inherited it from her—or maybe she inherited it from me. Maybe we pass it back and forth

The difference is I'm aware of it. That's not always a plus. Knowing why you do what you do doesn't guarantee you can stop it. I've been known to envy my mother's clue-free determination.

Speaking of clue-free, I hadn't realized how much stuff I still had at my mother's place. Boxes of record albums, boxes of assorted paper. The albums went into Patrick's basement, the paper flew out to Seattle, there to join other old boxes of paper in a big happy reunion.

After Mom moved into Valley Terrace, it was time to remove everything that remained in her house, which was a great deal. Julie and Patrick were able to use much of the furniture, and Kim shipped home some items. I was, by my standards, restrained, spending only a minor fortune in shipping. I'll have you know Kim and I made many trips to the local equivalent of Goodwill, and when I went weak in the knees it was because I was so tired, not because I was fixing to snatch bags back from the donation bins.

During this period, Kim and I journeyed to Vermont together several times. She knew what she was in for, trying to clean out with me. In fact, I warned her how much of a trial this would be for me, sorting through our family's things. Kim worked in the kitchen and garage and other heavily laden areas, her practical nature and minimal sentimentality making her perfectly suited to the task.

I sat among the CDs, trying hard not to think about what Kim was pitching.

I was a nor'easter of emotions: fear at my tasks, frustration at my speed, admiration for Kim's abilities, gratitude for her patience, embarrassment at my shortcomings. In a scenario tailor-made for conflict, Kim rarely got crabby, and I rarely disagreed about what we parted with. We wisely avoided some decisions by shoving items into our luggage.

It's not that I wasn't useful. I did purge a sizeable portion of Mom's belongings, and I tried to be as helpful as possible with the necessities, like runs to the dumpster. In other words, I looked for places where I could compensate for Fred.

But it's a fact that if I'd had to tackle emptying the home alone, I'd be sitting there still. Since we had to sell the house to cover Mom's care, that would've been a problem. I picture my siblings explaining to the real estate agent, "The house comes with our sister. She can't decide whether to keep the Broadway albums."

In the middle of 2020, Mom's doctor put her on hospice. With her congestive heart failure, she became weaker and more difficult for the staff to get in and out of bed. She needed a higher level of care than Valley Terrace could provide, so Kim and Julie hunted for a nursing home, and you-know-who embarked on the paperwork and finances to get Mom into a facility in Concord, N.H., in May 2021.

Unless Mom proves indestructible, this will be her last stop. She's defied most expectations by living this long after a debilitating stroke. If she knew how expensive this dying by degrees has been, she'd be appalled. If she grasped how limited her life is and how little brain wattage remains to her, she'd be aghast. My own suspicion is she has nothing left now but instinct, and that instinct is to survive, which is probably true of most people, but hers was sharpened all those years ago as bombs and bodies fell around her.

Or she's hanging around for twice-daily desserts. Whatever.

I've been in a state of overwhelm-age since the stroke happened. The sadness and frustration at watching her go through this, knowing full well this is the worst thing that could've happened to her. Her mind has been taken, and to a higher degree than Fred took mine.

For almost six years, the only trips I've made have been to New England to visit her and see to her many needs. By any standard, I've devoted a lot of time to taking care of her and her affairs.

It's been emotionally grueling, but as a practical matter, it's also eaten up a lot of writing time. See, there's this book inside me. Perhaps I've mentioned it.

Chapter 60

Soon after Anne and I married in 2013, and Fred's demands on my time were stressing me, I told her I was extremely disappointed that she hadn't yet found a way to add hours to the day.

"I'm a traditionalist," she responded. I hooted.

If only our mutual dealings with Fred were always so light.

One evening, when she grew acutely frustrated with me for not having read some emails she sent with information she knew would interest me, I flashed back to Alex's frustration when I didn't read stories he'd written.

Owing to this unattractive habit of not reading things until I feel up to dealing with them, I'd now pissed off both men and women.

I also realized Fred had been my longest partner. Ugh. Well, there's no doubt he's been the most devoted.

In the same way that I was told to give my OCD a name in order to see it as separate from me, Anne knew from the OCD group that she needed to try to separate my condition from me. To recognize that's Fred talking, not Leslie.

I'm well aware that in the heat of the moment it's easier to count back from 100,000. In Greek.

We both got a reminder of how powerful Fred is in early 2014. Anne's sister and her new boyfriend were due to spend Sunday night at our place, so on Saturday Anne declared she wanted to straighten up the house. I took laundry and vacuum duty. Anne grappled with getting the kitchen in shape. I heard her heading outside. When she returned, I asked her why she'd gone outside. To take out the garbage and recycling, she said, like a perfectly reasonable human being.

Recycling? I'd taken it out two hours earlier. Good Lord, she'd already created that much more? Damn. What's going out? I asked her, and she spoke of packing material and other benign items. I was nervous, but I let it go.

Over the last year or so I'd almost always been the one to take out the recycling, allowing me to gaze at every item that went into the bin, so virtually nothing went out without my stamp of approval. But she had cleaning on her mind. It was her impulses against my, um, compulses?

I heard that bloody door open again. She'd created and taken out more recycling. This was too much. Literally. I asked what had gone. She recited a list. There was nothing important. But I wanted to check the bin anyway, in case she'd missed something in her recitation, in case . . . just in case.

I didn't go outside to check, knowing that might tip her over the edge. I vacuumed. I stewed.

It had already become a given that when Anne got a notion to clean up, I got nervous. But on this Saturday she was particularly industrious, sorting out the bits from our honeymoon we hadn't yet dealt with, pulling together foodstuffs she wanted to give her sister, filing papers. She was moving things, changing the landscape, and I got more and more anxious. I hung on, knowing I was soon to leave for a housesitting gig, and that since she'd be following to have dinner with me there, she'd have to stop all these disquieting goings-on.

The next morning, at my housesit, I tried not to think about her at our home, on her own, unchecked, unsupervised, plowing through who knew what. When we talked on the phone, she said she'd been at it for two hours already. On the drive home, I tried to steel myself. I hoped against hope that it had taken her two hours to make the guest bed. No. She was still in rearranging mode. My anxiety soared.

I found myself standing on a step stool, trying to stuff quilts she handed me into a closet.

"That's it," I snapped, throwing the quilts on the bed. "I've reached my limit."

She looked surprised, then her expression hardened. "Stop if you have to."

I had to. I was overwhelmed, and furious at her for relentlessly ratcheting up her cleaning when she could see how hard it was on me.

She was plenty furious herself. "Another partner," she spat, would be thrilled to come home and see how much organizing she'd done. "Another partner" would appreciate her efforts. I came mighty close to saying go ahead and search for that other partner, but managed to store the sentiment in the vicinity of my molars.

Before long I was headed back to the housesit, and Anne announced she wouldn't join me. "I have no desire to be around Fred or you."

Kind of mean, yes—but she gets credit for managing to separate Fred from me.

The next morning I felt the nerves return just walking into the house, now more worried about our relationship than the contents of the recycling bin. Not that I'd forgotten about the latter, of course.

I hoped she'd admit she'd been the hopped-up Martha Stewart I accused her of being yesterday. Instead this turned out to be the rare discussion where we couldn't find common ground. She was sorry only for having hurt my feelings. I tried to explain this situation had been harder than usual because her full-throttle attack came as a surprise, and it felt like she was choosing her sister over me by decluttering so fiercely though she could see what it was doing to me.

The more we talked the more I saw I didn't have much of a leg to stand on. It was all Fred. My acute nerves made me not just unhelpful, but an actual impediment. And for no good reason, just fear. Fear over things being thrown out, moved, lost. I was controlled by irrational fear. And the longer I sat there the more I wished I had a gun. I was worthless.

I can't say if winning the argument or my patheticness moved her, but she said, "I love you." I snapped back, "That's your bad luck." It wasn't to be snotty to her. Well, it mostly wasn't. It was an expression of how much I hated myself at that moment.

This was one of those times where I failed at separating myself from Fred. The problem is mine. The problem is me. All these years of trying to see Fred as my illness, not as me, and I'm still prone to sliding into a vat of self-loathing. Painful, unproductive and monotonous.

Sigh.

All right, back to Fred, my wife and me.

In order to keep the living room from becoming too messy, Anne had bought two containers to hold my unread newspapers and magazines. I agreed that when the piles within peeped over the edge, some of that paper would have to go. It did—right up to my office.

Memorably, I amassed a mound of newspapers still in plastic, and even I knew there was no hope I'd read them. But I couldn't pitch them without going through them, which would take hours. I knew someone who'd enjoy the task of speedily separating the plastic and paper and recycling the lot. When Anne dug in, I had to be upstairs, where I couldn't see or hear what she was doing. For all I know, it may've been the happiest day of her life.

Anne likes to set due dates, and I optimistically agree to them, but I've missed many a target, which only makes the both of us unhappy. I can't purge on someone else's schedule.

At one point, I set out to go through a lot of paperwork, and stationed a long red table in our bedroom to hold sorted piles. The table was on my side of the room, so it wouldn't be in Anne's way. It was definitely in the way of our dogs, but Red and Blue didn't complain at their beds being moved a few feet. Animals are much more amenable to living with Fred.

I sorted and organized and pitched, all the while reporting my progress to Travis. Ain't going to lie—it was slow going. But it was going. Just not fast enough for Anne, who grew tired of that table taking up space.

Over time, Anne became more and more of the opinion that I wasn't trying hard enough to fight Fred. She couldn't see sufficient tangible progress. A shame that I mainly hoard paper. If I were clearing out, say, toaster ovens, the progress would be more obvious.

Travis didn't agree with Anne. He knew I was making a real effort. He's seen his share of hoarders who can't or won't tackle their accumulations. But I wasn't married to him.

There were moments when I might've preferred to have been, but his husband would've objected.

I look back now at the years following my marriage to Anne, when we both had evolving relationships with Fred, and I find the thing I regret most isn't plugging up the bedroom with the red table, or throwing anxiety tantrums. My biggest Fred-related regret is surprisingly specific.

Anne was intimidated by crossword puzzles. For me, oddly, crosswords were the one thing I could still do quickly, unlike reading or writing or . . . anything. When Anne saw me doing them, she wanted in. So at night in bed we'd tackle one together. I was a scribe more than anything, writing in her answers. It was unsatisfying for me, even frustrating, that I couldn't exercise the one area of mastery I retained.

I told Anne I wanted to return to doing crosswords alone, and I hurt her feelings, and I still feel badly, and for the sake of the marriage I should've shut up and scribbled. My desire to hang on to the one thing Fred hadn't stolen from me was too strong.

In this case, Fred interfered in my relationship with something he hadn't done, rather than something he had. Clever prick.

Anne and I had met in 2007, and married six years later. After we got hitched, it soon enough became apparent to me that Fred was just one of our issues, not even our biggest. There's a shame he'll never live down.

I'm the sort of person who prefers to talk a problem out for hours until it's solved and everybody's happy. Ann, by contrast, views conflict as a danger to her. I realized that when we argued, I took the view that we both believed in us and would strive to be fair and open; she took the view that disagreement was a personal threat.

Why she felt the need to defend herself, well, that's her book. We went into couples therapy twice, and basically flunked both times. She felt she couldn't get what she needed from me—which was a relationship similar to the one she'd had with her first partner of many years—and I felt our relationship had become more adversarial than team-like. What I'd loved most about her, her large heart, had shrunk toward me. She'd pulled the same move as the Grinch, but in reverse.

She moved into the other bedroom. We agreed to give couples therapy a third try. God, I didn't want to fail, not just because of my own perfection piece, but because we'd been activists for the right to marry, and how embarrassing to get hitched only to divorce.

One weekend, Anne changed her mind and declared we were done, and I had to get out of the house. Over the next couple of months Anne gave me, I felt shock, humiliation, anger . . . and utter panic at dealing with all my stuff. I got rid of a fair bit, but the bulk went to my sister's, and I was never so glad for the small structure next to Kim's house that thankfully was more suited to storage than anything else.

Each day I sorted clutter. Each day I grew frustrated with how much I had, and how hard all of it was to part with. I resorted to listing in my journal individual items of clothing and books I was giving away, so there'd be a record of what I'd had, which made parting with things easier. When I moved out on Oct. 1, 2018, I still had stuff left behind. I returned to walk Red and Blue daily, and deal with more of my crap.

I have no scientific data, but I'm willing to bet most hoarders are anti-divorce.

I initially moved in with a friend, then, to Fred's glee, had to move a couple more times over the next two years. I was never sure where I was or where my stuff was, but Fred I knew to be firmly in paradise.

As Anne and I underwent the divorce process and I looked back, I realized what a problem managing her anger toward me had been for her, and for us. I said so to Anne, and as I braced for a testy response, she shocked me senseless by agreeing. Cheers to her for the breakthrough. I just wish it had come sooner.

During our contentious final period together, I asked Anne why she didn't attend the OCD group with me anymore. "Because I realized you're not going to get better," she replied. When I reminded her of this post-split, she couldn't believe she'd said it, and apologized. But she did say it, and even before the decision to divorce, I knew I was alone in this fight.

That is, as alone as I can be with Fred always hanging around.

Thinking about Anne recently, more than two years after we separated, I felt such sadness that she didn't get help to deal with that corrosive anger. I realized I would've loved the chance to say to her, "I appreciate so much you doing this hard and scary work." Then I realized how much I would've loved hearing that from her.

Sometimes I think that the only successful couples are those whose mental and emotional shortcomings align in some way. By that logic, I should find someone with attention deficit disorder, who'd cherish how my checking covers for her inattention. Or perhaps I should seek out a nice agoraphobe who, unable to leave the house, loves that my hoarding means there's always something around to read.

Chapter 61

Following my split with Anne, I became more involved in the Seattle OCD and Hoarding Disorder Support Group, which pleased group chieftains Pam and Fred, who induced me to lead the small group for hoarders that meets following the large-group presentation.

We usually start our breakout group by reporting how we did with the goals we set at last month's meeting. Then we chat about the presentation or other pertinent matters, like where, in addition to Goodwill, stuff can be donated. Then we set new goals.

As a leader, I'm a hard-ass. Okay, I prefer to think of myself as patient but firm. I keep an eye on the clock, try to head off conversational tangents and make sure newbies or persons in particular distress get the airtime they need.

When it comes to setting goals, I'm all about keeping it real. Years ago at the meetings, I took it to heart when psychologists emphasized the importance of setting attainable goals. I've noticed how new attendees, giddy with having found folks who understand them, sometimes set overly ambitious goals. I'll find myself thinking, "If you could clear out two rooms in a month, sweetie, you wouldn't be here."

It's deeply unhelpful to start the process by failing. A person will feel worse than she already does. So I gently offer my mantra: "Does that feel doable?" The newbie might start out by—ironically—buying a book on hoarding, or looking for a therapist or decluttering one corner of her kitchen table. Rome wasn't purged in a day.

The experience of participating in the hoarding group has made one thing clear to me: I wish I'd invested in shredders.

After a meeting in early 2020, one woman bemoaned the fact that her shredder was busted. I responded that mine was, too. We who hoard paper, and try to do something about it, send shredders to early graves. If our shredders are broken, we run the risk of becoming immobile. Which might start to feel too comfy.

Sometimes before an appointment with Travis, the EBT Center has me fill out online questionnaires, designed to assess my current level of OCD and hoarding. Concerning the latter, one questionnaire asks practical questions, like, over the past week, "How much of your home does clutter prevent you from using?" and "How distressing do you find the task of throwing things away?"

Travis is lucky I'm required to circle a number as my answer. Otherwise he'd be reading a dissertation.

The other hoarding questionnaire gets at the thoughts hoarders have clearly offered to researchers as reasons we do what we do. When deciding whether to throw something away during the past week, the questionnaire asks, to what extent did I have thoughts such as these: "Throwing away this possession is like throwing away a part of me," and "Saving this means I don't have to rely on my memory" and "I am responsible for the well-being of this possession."

You hear sentiments like these hinted at or expressed in the hoarding group. Several of us are unwilling to let something go unless we know it will be valued. Which is why I thought Goodwill was pretty canny a few years ago when it started using the phrase, "Someone's going to love your stuff."

At one meeting, a woman said she had decades of Christmas cards. She didn't want just to recycle them, so we suggested seeing if an elementary school could use them. Between cards and magazines, we're either a boon or a bane to first-grade teachers.

Getting rid of something can absolutely feel to me like losing a part of myself, and I know it does for others. Taking that hit each time you part with an item is, when you think about it, a lot to ask.

About a year ago, when my roommate was away, I emptied a box in the living room and sorted. I came across two ticket stubs from Seattle's LGBTQ film festival. I couldn't remember the movies, so I intended to recycle the tickets. However, I googled one of the titles, and was reminded that it was a Canadian coming-of-age film. Then I remembered plot details and read a review. I essentially relived the experience. By keeping the ticket I remembered the event. The stub brought back something pleasant that I'd completely forgotten, so couldn't hoarding be seen as a positive?

Consider that a rhetorical question.

Now I'll tell you about a recent experience that I call the Triumph of the Hoarder. As KS prepared to move to a new building about six years ago, we had a lot of stuff to go through. The business's belongings, obviously, but also possessions of clients who'd died. I spotted and snagged a handful of old pamphlets and magazines on Swedish America before they could be recycled. At first I thought they might be eBay material—a common thought/excuse for hoarders. They weren't, but being a history aficionado, I suspected they could be of value to Seattle's Nordic Museum.

And being a hoarder who adores getting stuff to where it will be appreciated, I gave it a shot.

The museum wound up accepting—yes, I say, accepting!— most of the ephemera. The museum was happy, and the late former owner would surely be pleased her collection didn't wind up destroyed. For me, it was a peak experience. Hoarding heaven.

Was it worth dragging the material through three homes in two years? Don't bother me with details.

Like everything else on the planet, the OCD group found itself impacted by the arrival of the coronavirus. We couldn't meet in person anymore, so we turned to meeting online. A savvy volunteer handled most of the technical aspects, thank goodness. My math and science phobias emphatically carried over to technology. If I'd had to transfer people from the larger meeting to the breakout groups, the process would've looked like a "Star Trek" episode where everyone's molecules go missing.

During the quarantine year, we decided to try an online experiment. Some of the hoarding group members had in the past conducted an occasional one-on-one decluttering session over the phone. The idea is both persons try tackling some aspect of their conglomerations while providing mutual support. We wanted to try doing the same thing, but with more people: a group purge.

There were a number of unknowns, like could I actually negotiate Zoom well enough to make this happen, and would individuals find the atmosphere conducive or oppressive? I succeeded in arranging the meeting and getting the invitation out to everyone, and people gamely showed up. I began by asking each person to share what they planned to work on, and when we reconvened a half hour later, we had a hit on our hands.

I don't know whether it's the non-judgmental atmosphere, the encouragement, the sense of mutual suffering, the social aspect or simply being forced to zero in on those stacks for a defined period, but for most of the people who've participated, these decluttering sessions have been productive. By popular demand, we added a second session, so now we meet online once a month for two 40-minute go-rounds.

Our hoarding sub-group birthed a hoarding sub-sub-group. If we continue this way, we really will be down to molecules.

During these sessions, while others wander away to work on some part of their domicile, I stay planted in front of the screen, generally going through mail. I remain rooted in case someone has a question or needs to vent. Participants have a mostly positive attitude. The other day I heard a pile fall and the owner didn't miss a beat, yelling "Tim-berrrr!"

I immediately recalled that hoarders have actually died under their piles of accumulations. But if you live in a world where death by paperwork is a possibility, you have to find your humor where you can get it.

Chapter 62

The past few years have been demanding. In addition to the ever-present Fred, I've dealt with my mother's care, gone through the divorce process, moved repeatedly, endured a pandemic and watched a narcissist nail American democracy to the cross.

The narcissist repeatedly reminded me how many people out there have serious mental or emotional conditions that are never officially diagnosed, let alone dealt with. My illnesses led me right into poverty; his illnesses led him right into the White House.

As you'd expect, COVID-19 has been rough on many with OCD. Travis mentioned a German study of sufferers wherein 72% reported worsened symptoms due to the coronavirus. The hand-washers have had a hell of a time.

Yet some people with OCD have seen symptoms lessen. Staying at home has amounted to what Travis called "a sanctioned avoidance of triggers." If you normally exhaust yourself at the office by trying to hide your rituals, well, not going into work took care of that.

I felt during the pandemic that the planet caught up to me: You're anxious? Welcome to my world. Have a Life Saver.

Because of the type of work we do, KS stayed open the entire time. We staggered our shifts so fewer people would be in the office at once, and each morning I disinfected key surfaces. I sensed my co-workers had reached my regular level of anxiety. I felt like the calmest one among us. I wanted a crown.

My unlikely pseudo-serenity made me think of the wonderful Jean Kerr observation, "If you can keep your head when all about you are losing theirs, it's just possible you haven't grasped the situation." But I did grasp it. I knew people who died. I simply already lived at the pitch of anxiety where much of the world's population now found itself. As another client put it to Travis, "I've been training for this my whole life."

Not usually what's meant by pandemic-readiness, but there you are.

I know of one positive to come out of the COVID period. If the Seattle OCD and Hoarding Disorder Support Group hadn't been forced onto Zoom, we hoarders wouldn't have thought of virtual gatherings to declutter. I assume these will continue, even after we're able to hold large in-person meetings again, and that's a useful thing.

Another positive, strictly through the skewed lens of a hoarder, is during the pandemic nobody expected to be allowed into another's home. Soon we'll have to return to an unfortunate regimen of excuses and lies to keep family, friends, workmen and landlords from entering and seeing the truth. That whole process will have some hoarders looking back on the quarantine as the good old days.

As challenging as these years have been, I recently received a reminder that things could be worse. While leading the purging sessions, I noticed that one of our number wasn't getting anything out of them. It developed that Gail, in addition to hoarding disorder and OCD, also has attention deficit hyperactivity disorder (ADHD).

Nobody should have to battle that many letters of the alphabet.

I volunteered to go to her home and nudge her into action. It turned out her house, which she grew up in, was so packed with stuff, her own and that of her late parents, also hoarders, that there's one path through the place, and some rooms can't be entered. The outside is cluttered and overgrown. I told her what I'd want to hear—that I wouldn't throw out anything without her approval—but the speed at which she allows me to purge suggests we'll finish during the reign of Pope Margaret Beatrice II.

On my most recent visit, I stood near the road, in hand-to-hand combat with blackberry vines, when a woman walked by. She said it was nice of me to help Gail, thereby establishing that the neighborhood has an accurate idea of the situation. She added, "You're a good soul."

The compliment flustered me. Are you being thoughtful if you're acting out of the most basic empathy? Besides, in all honesty, I get a charge out of filling up Gail's recycling bin. It's always easier to cope with someone else's accumulations than your own. Which makes me think our hoarding group should consider another new idea: Each of us goes to another's home and declutters.

No. There might be bloodshed.

On that same visit, Gail said to me with real understatement, "I'm not a fighter." She survives her conditions; she doesn't battle them. Five years ago, after the death of her mother, she left her husband and her home several hours south, with the intention of moving into the family home long enough to clean it out. She's still there. The stuff is still there. Her husband still lives hours away.

As awful as OCD and hoarding are, and yes, I do carry a third issue in depression, I'm nonetheless grateful I don't have an additional condition like ADHD further bogging down my brain, the way Gail and others do. They live with a bonanza of burdens.

I should mention that if I did have another mental disorder to pair with Fred, I'd feel obliged to call it Wilma.

Chapter 63

Gail attends a second local hoarding group, and she told me that outfit doesn't use the word "hoarder," but rather "person who hoards." I admit it: at first I giggled at the tortured semantics. But I get that the reasoning is the same as naming your OCD—to separate yourself from the condition—so I'll have to consider proceeding with this approach for our group.

As to how I need to proceed with my life, that's clear to me. Finally. Over the many years, I've tried denial, minimizing, medications, therapy, alternative therapy, and nothing succeeded in ridding me of Fred. OCD and hoarding disorder are lifetime sentences for innocent people. The trick isn't making the conditions go away; it's managing them.

On the hoarding front, I've settled into spending 10 minutes a day, most days of the week, culling. I can't claim my apartment is now devoid of clutter. Far from it. I'm flanked by boxes right this minute. But I now have a positive habit ingrained in me that keeps, for instance, the mail from growing into a mountain range. Travis believes maintenance is critical. If you can't purge willy-nilly, at least you can keep the situation from getting worse.

Hardly the stuff of lofty dreams, but at age 57, pragmatism is the order of the day.

Because prodigious growth in my emails alarmed me, I decided to try to clear out five of those a day. So my almost-daily efforts are five emails and 10 minutes of general sorting, which is why I refer to them as the 5&10, or the Five-and-Dime or the Woolworth's Special.

On an irregular basis, I set aside several hours for a substantial run at the clutter. A few years ago, at the suggestion of my then-psychiatrist, I purged under the influence: I took Ritalin. It's proven useful for some hoarders—whoops, I mean people who hoard—and I found on that one occasion it helped keep me focused on the job.

I'm committed to reducing my stacks and piles, to be less burdened, so Ritalin may figure in going forward. I still don't love taking pharmaceuticals, but I won't turn my nose up at something that works for me. And I'm sure Karen, my present shrink, will have other suggestions that I'll want to shoot down but shouldn't.

Ritalin distinctly didn't work for me months after that first attempt. On the first try I took it to combat hoarding; the second time I took it to combat OCD. I popped a pill ahead of writing and performing other mental tasks. I lusted for the same focusing effect, but the Ritalin accomplished the opposite. My brain became fuzzy. I tried to write a check for my mother's caregivers, and my mind felt like an echo chamber as I went over it and over it. That "click" that I yearn for, the moment when I know I've done something right, felt even further away than normal, apparently having skipped off to the Solomon Islands.

Fred had seen me get some benefit from the med—no way that would happen again on his watch. How could he face his friends?

I told Travis I felt like I had enough in place to deal with the hoarding, and now we needed a plan for the OCD. Unfortunately, he came up with one.

When putting together a deposit at work, an occasion where Fred does love to flex his muscles, I now aim to check each step no more than three times. I'd be lying if I said I always succeed. Sometimes the need is so great, the conviction that I might've messed up so strong. But most of the time I stick to it, and the result is often a hunk of fear that I simply must sit with.

Yes, I could've made a mistake. The amount in that line might be wrong. Maybe I failed to list all the reimbursements. Perhaps I printed the receipt with disappearing ink. I have no choice but to languish with the doubt. When I've completed every step—so far as I know—I assess my level of nerves and write down that SUDS score, then keep checking with myself until the score is cut in half.

Since I began actively trying to sit with the possibility that I screwed up and not fix the anxiety by checking, I've had the occasional second where the desire to check isn't so strong. I hesitate to admit that, in case it was just wishful thinking, rather than a sign of improvement.

This week I worked on a deposit where no part of the process felt right, or even all that familiar. This would normally be grounds for panic and extensive checking, but it occurred to me this could be an indication that I was actually getting somewhere. Fred fears I'm not checking enough and he might lose me, so he strikes back by making me want to check even more. I upped my game, so he upped his.

I'm not sure if we're playing poker or Crazy Eights, but I'm sure he's the one in dark glasses.

I'm trying to apply the rule of checking only three times in all aspects of my work at the KS office. Again, I don't always succeed, but I try. In our line of work, my colleagues and I see plenty of drama, and though they all know I have OCD, they don't know of the new drama going on inside me each day.

I should tell them and charge admission to the office.

Whether I can apply this rule to my writing remains to be seen. That's the most important thing in my life, so Fred will fight me with everything he has. I've gingerly tried it when writing blog posts, and have largely succeeded. I haven't tried it while writing this book, I think because I started writing it nine years ago, when I was firmly rooted in the old ways.

Which is precisely why I should apply the rule, but gimme a break. Since I'm actually about to finish this book, and have proved I can do it, I pledge to allow only three checks on my next book.

I don't know which part of that sentence is scarier, "only three checks" or "next book."

I intend to keep working with Travis, who, mercifully, knows how to navigate between being demanding but not so demanding I want to murder him. I'll continue to attend the OCD group, and lead the breakout group for people who hoard, as well as the breakout group's breakout group for those who want to attempt to purge. Being among people who fight this fight is grounding, and I benefit from the variety of experts' perspectives. I'm pleased that I can help others battle their Freds when I lead the groups—and leading them in orderly fashion might be a sop to my perfectionistic OCD, but what the hell.

During a recent online session with Travis, I told him how writing this book has helped clarify for me who Fred is, how much he's taken from me and what I need to do about him going forward. Travis approvingly listed all the efforts I'm making these days to battle OCD and hoarding, adding, "If Anne could see you now."

I laughed. But if she could, I don't think it would matter. She needed big results, and wasn't in a place in her life where she had the patience for the process. Red and Blue, on the other hand, were loaded with patience. If I'm able to bring stability and income to this life of mine, it's not a lavish home or an expensive car I want. It's a dog. Who knows how to walk around boxes.

For there will still be some. I don't expect miracles—not anymore. I'll always have Fred. It's taken me all this time to absorb that my only way of reducing his impact is to do the things that scare me the most. I have to put in that fear time in order to reach a place where he has less control of me. I must do exactly what any functioning human being would avoid: force myself into situations over and over, all day long, that terrify me. And I must keep doing that, not slack off as I did years ago.

Here I am, pushing 60 and throwing down the gauntlet. I'm scared. Fred's smirking. Place your bets.

Whatever the outcome, it hasn't been nice knowing Fred. At last! A fact I'll never need to check.

Author Bio

As a freelance writer, and despite Fred's best efforts, Leslie Robinson has written for a variety of local and national publications, including the *Chicago Tribune,* the *Dallas Morning News, The Philadelphia Inquirer, Games* magazine, *World Tennis* and *Cosmopolitan.* For about a decade, she wrote a humor column called "General Gayety" for LGBTQ publications across the country, and now blogs at www.generalgayety.com.

You can reach Leslie—or drop Fred a fan letter—at: LeslieandFred13@gmail.com.

Made in United States
North Haven, CT
06 October 2022

25091748R00109